CHECKLISTS FOR VOCABULARY STUDY

RICHARD YORKEY

Longman

New York

CHECKLISTS FOR VOCABULARY STUDY

Library of Congress Cataloging in Publication Data

Yorkey, Richard.
  Checklists for vocabulary study.

  Includes index.
  1. English language—Textbooks for foreigners.
2. Vocabulary.   I. Title.
PE1128.Y57   428.1   81-569
ISBN   0-582-79767-5   AACR2

First printing 1981

Sponsoring Editor: Arley Gray
Project Editor: Dorothy Niemczyk

Cover and Text Design: Antler and Baldwin Inc.
Illustrations: Gregory Stewart

 Longman
95 Church Street
White Plains, New York 10601

Distributed in the United Kingdom by Longman Group Ltd., Longman House, Burnt Mill, Harlow, Essex CM20 2JE, England, and by associated companies, branches and representatives throughout the world.

9 10-AL-9594939291

Contents

To the Student

There is certainly no need to tell you how important vocabulary is. One purpose of these lists is to give you many of the most common and useful words that you are likely to need. Another purpose is to put these words into their patterns of formation, to make them easier to learn.

When you think about vocabulary, you probably think only of the *meaning* of words. Meaning, of course, is important; but so also is the *form* of words. This book emphasizes not only the meaning of many common words in English but the different forms of these words as well. For example, take the verb *to imagine;* the nouns *imagination* and *image;* the adjectives *imaginative, unimaginative* and *imaginary* and the adverb *imaginatively.* Part of knowing any word in English is knowing the use and meaning of its different forms.

It may help you to learn the correct form of words if you understand a few ways in which many common words in English are formed:

I. All English words have a *root.* This is the form which carries the basic meaning of the word. It can be changed by adding a form at the beginning (a *prefix*) or a form at the end (a *suffix*). The root form may be any one of the four parts of speech (a verb, noun, adjective or adverb). Again, use *to imagine* as an example. One meaning is something like "to form a picture or idea in the mind" (in other words, *an image*). One who can do this is *imaginative;* one who cannot do this, one who has no *imagination,* is *unimaginative.* Something that is only in the mind and not real is *imaginary.* These changes can be described either in a kind of formula or as a diagram. Note that spelling changes often result. They are sometimes very little (for example: *imagine + -ation = imagination*) but sometimes they are great (for example: *conceive + -tion = conception*).

Here are the words we can form with the verb *imagine* and its prefixes and suffixes.

A. ROOT VERB + SUFFIX	= NOUN	
-imagin-	+ -ation	= imagination	imagin|ation
B. ROOT VERB + SUFFIX	= ADJECTIVE	
-imagin-	+ -ary	= imaginary	imagin|ary

C. ROOT VERB + SUFFIX   = ADJECTIVE

   -imagin-   + -ative   = imaginative   imagin|ative

D. ADJECTIVE + SUFFIX   = ADVERB

   imaginative + -ly   = imaginatively   imagin|ative|ly

E. PREFIX   + ADJECTIVE = NEGATIVE ADJ.

   un-   + imaginative = unimaginative   un|imagin|ative

F. PREFIX   + ADVERB   = NEGATIVE ADV.

   un-   + imaginatively = unimaginatively   un|imagin|ative|ly

II. Here are some of the common prefixes you will find in the check-lists:

   A. *un-* / *in-* / *im-* / *ir-* / *il-* / *non-* / *dis-* / = negative

      1. *un-*   unimportant, uncommon

      2. *in-*   insane, inconvenient

      3. *im-*   impossible, improper

      4. *ir-*   irreligious, irresponsible

      5. *il-*   illegal, illogical

      6. *non-* non-stop, non-verbal

      7. *dis-* disagree, dishonorable

   B. *re-* / = again

      1. *re-* rewrite, reproduce, rearrange

III. Here are some of the more common suffixes you will find. They are listed here by the way in which they change the part of speech. You should become familiar with these. Although there is no sure way to know which suffix is used with which root, listen carefully and notice as you read. Develop eyes and ears that are aware of the natural uses of these forms.

   Also, note that spelling changes in the root words are sometimes necessary when you add a suffix. Here are some of them:

   dropping final *e*: imagin*e* – imaginative; argu*e* – arg*u*ment

   changing *y* to *i*: happ*y* – happ*i*ly; beaut*y* – beaut*i*ful

changing a final consonant: atten*d* — atten*t*ive; explo*de* —
explo*s*ive

As you work with the checklists, be sure to pay attention to all spelling changes.

A. To make nouns

1.	VERB + *-ment*	argument, disappointment, payment
2.	VERB + *-tion/-sion*	invention, confusion, discussion
3.	VERB + *-ation/-ition*	limitation, composition, declaration
4.	VERB + *-ance/-ence*	dependence, insurance, reference
5.	VERB + *-or/-er*	owner, manager, player, visitor
6.	NOUN + *-ship*	friendship, leadership, membership
7.	NOUN + *-hood*	neighborhood, adulthood
8.	ADJECTIVE + *-ness*	kindness, thickness, foolishness
9.	ADJECTIVE + *-ty/-ity*	cruelty, equality, loyalty

B. To make adjectives

1.	NOUN + *-less*	careless, hopeless, thoughtless
2.	NOUN + *-ful*	doubtful, peaceful, plentiful
3.	NOUN + *-al*	formal, original, accidental
4.	NOUN + *-y*	healthy, guilty, hungry
5.	NOUN + *-ous/-ious/-eous*	dangerous, glorious, courageous
6.	VERB + *-able/-ible*	agreeable, favorable, convertible
7.	VERB + *-ive*	attractive, progressive, selective
8.	PAST PARTICIPLE	wasted, frightened, broken

Note that many but not all past participles can be used as adjectives. Those that are commonly used are included in the checklists (*an abandoned child, a devoted friend*). Many others may be possible (for example, *an investigated idea*) but they are either uncommon or awkward; these are not included in the checklists.

C. To make verbs

1. NOUN/ADJECTIVE + *-en* hasten, soften, threaten, weaken

D. To make adverbs

1. ADJECTIVE + *-ly* safely, quickly, dangerously

Note these two small points:

a. A very few adjectives also end in -*ly*. For example:

Our teacher is a *friendly* person.
My father reads the *daily* newspaper.

b. Several adverbs do *not* end in -*ly*. For example:
Hippolito has to work hard.

Note that *Hippolito works hard* means that he puts in a lot of effort. *Hippolito hardly works* means that he works very little.

Note also that not all adjectives can or should be made into adverbs. For example, although *wealthy* - *wealthily* or *valuable* - *valuably* are possible formations (and may be given in dictionaries), it is difficult to think of an adverbial use that would sound natural. In these checklists, only the common, most useful adverbs are included.

How to Use This Book

All the words in this book have been identified as frequent words[1] beyond the intermediate level of the 2000 most common words in English,[2] so you can be sure that the words in these checklists are important for you to know.

You may already know many of these words. If so, do not waste time looking them up in a dictionary. Many of these words you may not know. If not, you should learn them because they are very important for English beyond the intermediate level. Here are some suggestions for do-it-yourself study and checking to find out which words you need to learn.

1. Look down the words on the checklist quickly. Put a check beside any word whose meaning or form you are not sure of.

2. Look up in a dictionary those words that you have checked. Study the meanings, all the possible forms of the word, and whatever sample sentences your dictionary gives. Read the *entire* entry carefully, and also be sure to look at the words above and below the entry. Very often these words are related in some way.

[1]Jean Praninskas, *American University Word List* (London: Longman, 1972).
[2]Michael West, *A General Service List of English Words* (London: Longman, 1953).

3. You will need a *good* standard English-English dictionary, *not* a bilingual dictionary. The *Longman Dictionary of Contemporary English* is highly recommended because (1) it has been prepared especially for students of English as a second or foreign language, (2) it includes many sentences as examples of meaning and usage, (3) it includes both American and British spelling, pronunciation, meanings and usage and (4) it is up-to-date.

4. When you think you have a good idea of the meanings, the forms and the various uses of the words in the checklist, do the exercises which immediately follow the list. Each exercise has 25 items. Do these without using a dictionary or looking back at the checklist. When you have finished, check your answers with the Answer Key at the back of the book. Be especially sure that your spelling is correct.

5. Review the meaning or the forms of any word that you had wrong. First, be sure to use the full resources of your dictionary. Read the entry and examples carefully. If you still do not understand, ask your teacher or a native speaker of English.

6. When you finish all the checklists, again review the words. Then check yourself by taking the Review Tests at the end.

Checklist 1

In this list each noun is based on a verb to which *-ion* can be added. Other noun forms are also given. Either *-ion* is added directly to the verb (for example, *abstract - abstraction*) or the final *-d(e)* or *-t(e)* is changed to *-s(s)* (for example, *invade - invasion* or *emit - emission*).

VERBS	NOUNS	ADJECTIVES	ADVERBS
abstract	abstraction abstract	abstract	
assert	assertion	assertive	
comprehend	comprehension	comprehensible incomprehensible	
conclude	conclusion	(in)conclusive	(in)conclusively
construct reconstruct	construction reconstruction	(un)constructive	(un)constructively
contract	contraction contract	contractual	
contradict	contradiction	contradictory	
convert	conversion convert convertibility	converted convertible	
edit	edition editor	edited	
emit	emission		
exclude	exclusion	exclusive	exclusively
exert	exertion		
expand	expansion expanse	expanded	

instruct	instruction instructor	instructive	
invade	invasion invader		
predict	prediction (un)predictability	(un)predictable	
project	projection project	projected	
reject	rejection reject	rejected	
restrict	restriction	(un)restrictive (un)restricted	
select	selection	selective	selectively

Exercise 1

Select the one word from the four choices that best completes the sentence. Write *the correct form of the word* on the line at the right. The first sentence is done for you as an example. When you finish the exercise, check your answers with the Answer Key. Be sure your spelling is correct.

Last year a fortune teller _____ that Billy would grow up to be a famous lion tamer.

<u>predicted</u>

contradict   exert   predict   reject

1. At the _____ of the speech, the audience cheered wildly.

    _____

conclude   project   comprehend   convert

2. John told his wife that she was the most intelligent woman in the world and she didn't _____ him.

    _____

invade   emit   abstract   contradict

3. Yesterday Grandpa Gomez _____ a doghouse for his grandson's dog.

    _____

conclude   construct   exert   exclude

4. For many years the government has _____ the sale of alcohol to people twenty-one years old and over.

   predict   restrict   select   exert

   _____

5. Chris learned how to drive after only ten hours of _____.

   instruct   construct   exert   abstract

   _____

6. The English teacher was unhappy when a publisher _____ his novel because of its bad grammar and faulty punctuation.

   expand   assert   reject   contradict

   _____

7. The teacher's wife said that she would not correct her husband's mistakes or in any way _____ the book for him.

   convert   edit   instruct   select

   _____

8. Every winter Miami Beach is _____ by thousands of tourists.

   invade   reconstruct   exclude   restrict

   _____

9. Although Senator Smith _____ all her influence, the president did not agree to make Mr. Smith the ambassador to Iceland.

   convert   exert   comprehend   emit

   _____

10. Alice was surprised but pleased when she was _____ from 73 other women to be the Beauty Queen.

    select   conclude   project   emit

    _____

11. The word *beauty* is an _____ noun.

    exclusive   abstract   edited   instructive

    _____

12. The weather bureau's _____ for a sunny day was not very accurate. It's raining now.

    emit   select   predict   exclude

    _____

13. If a chimney is not kept clean, it may _____ a lot of black smoke.

    assertion   contraction   exclusion   emission

    _____

14. The development of the atomic bomb during World War II was a secret _____.

    project   edition   contract   assertion

15. The guilty man tried to _____ his innocence.

    comprehend   assert   emit   invade

16. *It's, you're* and *I'll* are examples of _____.

    contract   convert   expand   project

17. Once elected, the mayor's actions were clearly _____ to her campaign promises.

    conversion   expansion   selection   contradiction

18. The Chicago Chinese Checkers Club is so _____ that it has only forty members.

    reject   exclude   conclude   contract

19. After the two merchants agreed on the price, they signed a _____.

    reject   project   contract   construct

20. Extreme variations of temperature cause metal to _____ and contract.

Complete each of the following sentences with another form of the underlined word. The first is done for you as an example. Check your answers with the Answer Key.

A new _____ of Dickens' novels has been <u>edited</u> by his grandson.   <u>edition</u>

21. Ms. Fox is an <u>instructor</u> who cannot understand why her students do not enjoy her _____.

22. Although the enemy _____ was successful at first, the <u>invaders</u> were finally thrown back.

23. Many Americans do not want to _____ from the Fahrenheit scale to the Celsius scale, but the <u>conversion</u> may take place anyway.

24. Paula does not <u>comprehend</u> English very well, but her _____ is much better than her speaking.

25. When the Empire State Building was _____ in 1931, it was the tallest <u>construction</u> in the world.

4

Checklist 2

In this list the final *-e* of the verb is dropped and *-ion* is added to form the noun.

VERBS	NOUNS	ADJECTIVES	ADVERBS
attribute	attribution attribute	attributive	attributively
communicate	communication	(un)communicative	
concentrate	concentration	concentrated	
constitute	constitution constituent	(un)constitutional	
contribute	contribution contributor	contributory	
cooperate	cooperation cooperative	(un)cooperative	cooperatively
coordinate	coordination	(un)coordinated	
correlate	correlation	correlated	
create	creation creativity creator	(un)creative	creatively
demonstrate	demonstration demonstrator	(un)demonstrative demonstrable	demonstratively demonstrably
devastate	devastation	devastated	
devote	devotion devotee	devoted devout	devotedly devoutly
dictate	dictation dictator dictatorship	dictatorial	

dominate	domination		
	dominance	dominant	
predominate	predominance	predominant	predominantly
duplicate	duplication	duplicate	
	duplicate		
estimate	estimation		
	estimate	estimated	
execute	execution		
	executioner		
	executive	executive	
formulate	formulation		
	formula		
frustrate	frustration	frustrating	
		frustrated	
illustrate	illustration	illustrated	
	illustrator	illustrative	
initiate	initiation		
	initial	initial	initially
	initiative		
institute	institution	institutional	institutionally
	institute		

Exercise 2

Complete each of the following sentences with an appropriate word form of one of the verbs below. You may use a verb, noun, adjective or adverb form. Note that there are more verbs than necessary. Check your answers with the Answer Key. Be sure your spelling is correct.

communicate	correlate	estimate
constitute	devastate	execute
contribute	devote	initiate
coordinate	duplicate	institute

1. Billy's _____ of twenty-five cents was appreciated by the Red Cross.

   _____

2. We are now only at the _____ stage of space exploration.

   _____

3. Please _____ to the nearest hundred dollars what my car repairs will cost.

   _____

4. Uncle Edward shows his great _____ to his wife by serving her breakfast in bed every morning.

   _____

5. In swimming it is necessary to _____ the movement of the arms and legs.

   _____

6. English is an important language for international _____.

   _____

7. John made _____ keys for the house: one for his wife and one for himself.

   _____

8. There is a probable _____ between smoking and cancer.

   _____

9. San Francisco was _____ by a terrible earthquake and fire in 1906.

   _____

10. Monique is studying business administration because she wants to be a highly paid _____ in a large company.

    _____

Select the one word from the four choices that best completes the sentence. Write *the correct form of the word* on the line at the right.

11. Karen is such a _____ of rock music that she owns all the best records, knows all about the latest stars and attends every concert she can.

    _____

    devotee   dictator   constituent   demonstrator

12. A magnifying glass will _____ sunlight so that just a small point of light is hot enough to start a fire.

    _____

    creation   dictation   concentration   formulation

13. Mr. Cochran has a very _____ personality in class. All the students are afraid of him and do not question anything he says.

    _____

    attribute   dominate   constitute   illustrate

14. John didn't really know his mother-in-law very well; therefore, it was unfair of him to _____ an opinion of her personality.

    formulate   coordinate   constitute   estimate

15. Some members of the church are more _____ than others and attend services every week.

    create   coordinate   predominate   devote

16. Thomas Edison _____ his success as an inventor to 10% inspiration and 90% perspiration.

    devote   execute   attribute   institute

Each of the following groups of sentences is preceded by a verb. For each sentence in the group, decide on the correct word form — verb, noun, adjective or adverb — and write it on the line at the right. The first is done for you as an example.

to demonstrate

    Two plus two equals five is _____ false.   demonstrably

17. A salesperson gave a _____ of how the vacuum cleaner works.

18. During the antiwar protest, one of the _____ was injured by a police officer.

19. The _____ child warmly kissed his grandparents.

to frustrate

20. Ms. Thomas is probably unaware of her students' _____ with English grammar.

21. The enemy attack was _____ by the arrival of a large military force of planes and ground troops.

22. It is _____ to study so many new vocabulary words and then not be tested on them.

to initiate

23. The management of the company _____ discussions with the labor union about a new contract.

24. Carolyn showed great _____ by going out after her classes every day and looking for a job.

25. The doctor knew the man's name was Peabody, but she couldn't remember his first _____.

Checklist 3

Like the preceding list, in this list the final *-e* of the verb is dropped and *-ion* is added.

VERBS	NOUNS	ADJECTIVES	ADVERBS
integrate	integration	integrated integral	
disintegrate	disintegration	disintegrated	
investigate	investigation investigator		
isolate	isolation isolationism isolationist	isolated	
migrate	migration	migratory migrant	
immigrate	immigration immigrant		
emigrate	emigration emigrant		
motivate	motivation motive	motivational motivated motivating	
obligate oblige	obligation	obligatory obliging obliged	
participate	participation participant	participatory	
radiate	radiation radiance radius	radiant radial	radiantly
segregate desegregate	segregation desegregation	(un)segrated desegregated	
stimulate	stimulation stimulus stimulant	stimulating	
subordinate	(in)subordination	(in)subordinate	

The rest of Checklist 3 includes miscellaneous nouns that end in
-tion or -sion.

deduce	deduction	deductive	deductively
expose	exposition exposure	expository (un)exposed	
impress	impression	(un)impressive impressionable	impressively
induce	induction	inductive	inductively
repress	repression	repressive	repressively
retain	retention	retentive	
revise	revision	revised	
supervise	supervision supervisor	supervisory	
suppress	suppression suppressor	suppressive	

Exercise 3

Complete each of the following sentences with an appropriate word
form of one of the verbs below. You may use a verb, noun, adjective or
adverb form. Note that there are more verbs than necessary. Check
your answers with the Answer Key. Be sure your spelling is correct.

assert	isolate	segregate
induce	motivate	stimulate
integrate	repress	subordinate
investigate	retain	supervise

1. Betty's _____ to become a lawyer does not seem
   to be very strong.   _____

2. The lawyer _____ his ideas loudly and clearly.   _____

3. When Mary heard a strange noise at three o'clock in the morning, she got up to _____ the cause.   _____

4. Drink coffee when you're sleepy; it's a good _____ and will help to keep you awake.   _____

5. I had to _____ my desire to laugh while being reprimanded by my supervisor.   _____

6. The army officer was surprised by the _____ behavior of the captain. There had never been a case of insubordination before.   _____

7. Because the workers were new and inexperienced, the manager of the factory had to watch them and _____ their work closely.   _____

8. To bring black and white children closer together and to provide equal opportunity, the United States has passed laws for the racial _____ of schools.   _____

9. Even at 87, John's mother-in-law has _____ her physical energy and youthful attitude.   _____

10. Heavy snowfall blocked the roads and _____ many towns in northern Japan from each other.   _____

Select the one word from the four choices that best completes the sentence. Write *the correct form of the word* on the line at the right.

11. If you saw a doctor leaving a house, you might _____ that someone in the house was ill.   _____

    deduce   repress   suppress   radiate

12. If you _____ yourself to sunlight for too long, you can get a serious sunburn.   _____

    stimulate   isolate   expose   induce

13. It is the _____ of parents to care for their children.   _____

    segregate   obligate   integrate   expose

14. The military government tried to _____ the revolution by imprisoning its leaders.   _____

    retention   emigration   revision   suppression

11

15. My grandparents _____ on their grandchildren the importance of honesty and hard work.   _____

    induce   supervise   impress   participate

16. Nuclear power plants must be carefully monitored so they do not emit harmful _____.   _____

    stimulate   radiate   retain   impress

17. The students voted Walter the most active and helpful _____ in the Red Cross campaign to raise $100,000.   _____

    stimulate   radiate   isolate   participate

Notice the difference in meaning between these words:

To immigrate means to come to and settle in another country.

To emigrate means to leave one's country and go to live in another country.

An immigrant is one who immigrates to (arrives in) another country.

An emigrant is one who emigrates from (leaves) his or her own country.

Thus, a citizen of Poland is an *emigrant* when he or she emigrates *from* Poland. He or she is an *immigrant* when he or she immigrates *to* Canada.

Migrant and *migratory* mean much the same thing, but *migrant* is usually used with human beings and *migratory* with animals; for example, *migrant workers* and *migratory birds*.

From the following five words, select the one that best completes each sentence. Write the word on the line at the right. Check your answers with the Answer Key.

emigrated   emigration   immigration
migration   immigrant

18. _____ to Canada is now more restricted than in the past.   _____

19. Reinhold's father is an _____ who came here from Switzerland in 1919.   _____

20. Many German intellectuals _____ from Germany and settled in the United States after the rise of Hitler.   _____

21. The Roman Empire was destroyed by the _____ of the Vandals, Goths and Visigoths across Europe.   _____

22. Since World War II, there has been very little
_____ from the Soviet Union.   _____

Although *deduction* and *induction* have other clearly separated meanings, their meanings as methods of logical reasoning are easily confused. Notice the difference:

Deduction is a method of reasoning that starts from a general principle or law and reaches a conclusion for a particular case. For example:

General law: The sun always rises in the east.

Particular case: This morning the sun rose over that mountain over there.

Conclusion: Therefore, that mountain over there must be in the east.

Induction is a method of reasoning that starts from a particular case and reaches a conclusion of a general principle or law. For example:

Day 1: That is the east over there and the sun is rising.

Day 2: That is the east over there and the sun is rising.

Day 3: That is the east over there and the sun is rising.
and so on . . . .

General law: In every example the sun rises in the east.

Conclusion: Therefore, the sun must always rise in the east.

These two words are easily confused, partly because deduction must start from a general law or principle that has been reached by induction. Remember that *induction* goes from the particular to the general, while *deduction* goes from the general to the particular. Using a form of either of these two words, complete the following sentences. Write *the correct form of the word* on the line at the right.

23. It may be an unpleasant fact to think about, but it
is not difficult to _____ that you will die, since all
human beings must die someday.   _____

24. When your teacher gives you many examples and
then asks you to draw some general conclusion,
he or she is using the _____ approach to learning.   _____

25. If you see that the street is wet in the morning,
you would _____ that it must have rained during
the night.   _____

13

Checklist 4

In this list, the noun is formed by adding *-ation, -ition, -ution* or *-ication* to the verb. Note the comments preceding each group.

To form the first five nouns, *-ation* is added directly to the verb without change.

VERBS	NOUNS	ADJECTIVES	ADVERBS
adapt	adaptation		
	adaptability	adaptable	
alter	alteration	(un)alterable	unalterably
confirm	confirmation	(un)confirmed	
conform	conformation		
	conformist		
	(non-conformist)		
	conformity		
interpret	interpretation		
misinterpret	misinterpretation		

To form the following nouns, the final *-e* of the verb is dropped and *-ation* is added.

compute	computation	computational	
computerize	computer	computerized	
condense	condensation	(un)condensed	
	condenser		
conserve	conservation	conservative	conservatively
	conservationism		
	conservationist		
console	consolation	consoling	

14

| derive | derivation | derivational | |
| | derivative | derivative | |

| restore | restoration | (un)restored | |

To form the following nouns, the final *-e* of the verb is dropped and *-ition* is added.

define	definition	(in)definite	(in)definitely
		undefined	
		definitive	definitively

| propose | proposition | | |
| | proposal | | |

The following verbs all end in *-fy* or *-ly.* To form the noun, the *-y* is changed to *-i* and *-cation* is added.

identify	identification	(un)identifiable	
	identity	identical	identically
imply	implication	implicit	implicitly
justify	justification	(un)justifiable	(un)justifiably
modify	modification	modifiable	
	modifier		
specify	specification		
	specificity	(un)specific	specifically

In the following group, each noun form is slightly changed before *-ation*, *-ition* or *-ution* is added.

| acquire | acquisition | acquisitive | |

administer	administration administrator	administrative	administratively
cease	cessation	incessant ceaseless	incessantly ceaselessly
denounce	denunciation		
evolve	evolution	evolutionary	
reveal	revelation		
revolt	revolution revolt	revolutionary revolting	
vary	variation variability variety	varied (in)variable various	(in)variably variously

Exercise 4

Each of the following groups of sentences is preceded by a verb. For each sentence in the group, decide on the correct word form – verb, noun, adjective or adverb – and write it on the line at the right.

to derive

1. John occasionally _____ a great deal of pleasure from taking long trips by himself. _____

2. The _____ of the word *grammar* is unusual and very interesting. _____

to imply

3. A young son seldom doubts his father's judgment. He has _____ faith in him. _____

4. Although the detective did not say so exactly, she _____ that the murderer was from London. _____

5. The teacher smiled, with the _____ that he didn't believe the boy's story about losing his homework on the way to school. _____

to identify

6. The customs officer at the border asked me to prove my citizenship by showing her some kind of _____. _____

7. The _____ of the killer was not revealed to the reader until the last page of the novel. _____

8. The twins were _____. No one could tell them apart. _____

Complete each of the following sentences with another form of the underlined word.

9. The candidate agreed to modify her speech, but her _____ did not satisfy many of the voters. _____

10. Our class includes a variety of students from _____ countries around the world. _____

11. By a process of evolution, many land animals _____ from animals in the sea. _____

12. Fujiko interprets Picasso's paintings in her own way. She refuses to accept her husband's _____. _____

13. Uncle Marco wants to restore his 1930 car, but Aunt Louisa doesn't want to pay for such an unnecessary _____. _____

Select the one word from the four choices that best completes the sentence. Write *the correct form of the word* on the line at the right.

14. The doctor's orders were very _____: take two pink pills every four hours, one yellow pill every six hours and two tablespoons of medicine before sleeping. _____

    specific   revolutionary   modifiable   restorative

15. Because André does not speak English, it will be necessary to _____ the speaker's remarks for him. _____

    confirmation   consolation   interpretation   justification

16. Parents do not need to state their love for their children too often or too loud. Their love is _____

17

in their daily way of helping and caring for them. _____

alter   imply   vary   condense

17. When you go to a new country, you must _____ yourself to many new and different customs. _____

adapt   alter   console   specify

18. The report was too long. The teacher asked the student to _____ it so it wouldn't be more than ten pages. _____

conserve   acquire   condense   denounce

19. By traveling, reading and studying, the scholar devoted all his time to the _____ of knowledge. _____

acquire   vary   restore   cease

20. The price of this suit was only $49.95, but the _____ to make it fit properly cost $30! _____

reveal   condense   derive   alter

21. Janice buys all the fashion magazines, and she always tries to dress in _____ with the latest styles. _____

confirm   conform   propose   vary

22. The presidential candidates regularly repeated what they would do to improve the economy, but the voters quickly tired of their _____ promises. _____

incessant   acquisitive   computational   derivational

23. Because of the fuel shortage in the world, it is necessary for everyone to _____ gasoline. _____

specific   conservative   computerized   acquisitive

24. Many women object to the use of the word *men* in the _____ that "all men are created equal." _____

propose   justify   adapt   compute

25. The date of our next test has been _____ postponed. Now we don't know when it will be given, or if it will be given at all. _____

identical   unidentifiable   indefinite   conservative

Crossword Puzzle 1

This puzzle contains 20 words from Checklists 1 through 4, plus other words that you probably already know. Solve the puzzle by filling in the blanks to complete the sentences.

ACROSS

2. The committee suggested several changes in the report and asked Bill to _____ it accordingly.
5. What time is _____ now?
7. If no one answers the telephone, you can _____ that no one is home.
10. He couldn't buy anything because he had _____ money.
11. If two people don't speak the same language, it is difficult for them to _____ with each other.
13. Many citizens were so angry that they wrote to the president to _____ the court's decision.
15. To assert something is to _____ it forcefully.
16. December 31 is the _____ of the year.
17. Before a book can be published, someone must _____ it.
19. This puzzle is easier than _____ puzzle.
21. Jack drove eight people to the party in his _____.
22. Mrs. Martin told her young children not to go too _____ the water.
23. Something that is lawful is _____.
24. When I _____ on the chair, it broke.
26. The military court voted to _____ the traitor by hanging.
27. Now there are laws regulating the amount of pollution that new cars can _____.
28. _____, I would like a glass of water.
30. _____, I don't want any ice in it.
31. During a discussion, only _____ person should speak at a time.
32. Let's _____ everyone's work so we can get it done quickly and efficiently.
36. In order to succeed you have to _____ a little effort.
37. According to the Bible, it took God only six days to _____ the world.

DOWN

1. Andrea wants to _____ a doctor when she grows up.
2. I'll help you if you'll help _____.

3. A single nuclear bomb could _____ everything in an area of at least a mile in diameter.

4. I thought the movie had already begun, but it hadn't started _____.

5. The army was waiting at the border, ready in case the enemy tried to _____.

6. You can leave now if you want _____.

8. Elizabeth is very pushy and always tries to _____ people.

9. To play chess well requires remarkable powers of _____.

11. As the gas becomes cool, it _____ into a liquid.

12. Because of his unforgivable behavior, Gerald has lowered himself in my _____.

14. Ellen Newkirk's initials are _____.

18. It is possible for two people to _____ the same poem in two different ways.

20. You may have _____ the time you need to solve this puzzle.

21. Old people usually don't like to _____ their daily routines too much.

25. Mike brought an _____ to chop the wood.

29. Gladys will have to _____ her dress if she wants it to fit her daughter.

30. There are _____ players on a baseball team.

33. Here are two cars you may like. _____ is cheap and the other is very expensive.

34. _____ looked at himself in the mirror.

35. The game begins _____ 7:30.

Crossword Puzzle 2

Use the following definitions and sentences to solve this crossword puzzle. All the words are the dictionary form of verbs from Checklists 1 through 4. Check your answers with the Answer Key.

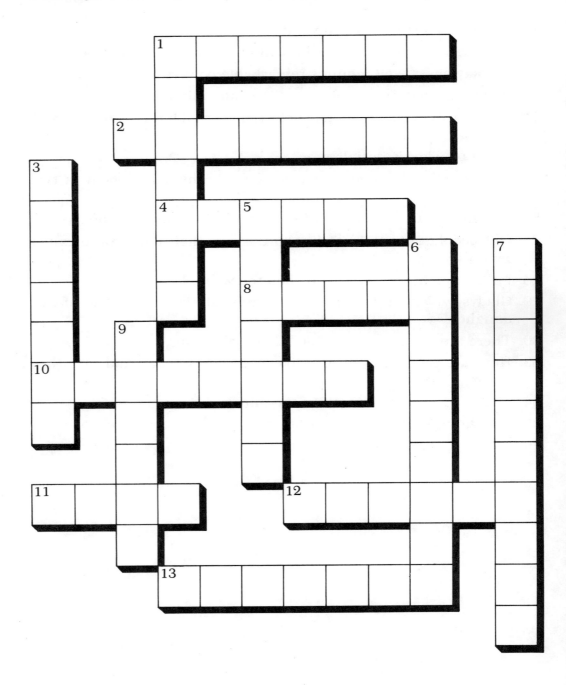

ACROSS

1. *to suggest; to put forward a plan for consideration.*
   The president intends to _____ a solution to the energy problem.

2. *to rule or control others by power or authority.*
   Even after his children left home, the father continued to _____ them by writing and telephoning his opinions.

4. *to increase in size.*
   If you heat metal, it will _____.

8. *to use physical strength or force of character; to make an effort.*
   Students usually _____ more effort just before exams.

10. *to limit; to keep within a certain space or amount.*
    The teacher asked the students to _____ their compositions to the past tense.

11. *to be different; to have qualities that are not the same as each other.*
    These apples _____ in quality from very good to very bad.

12. *to keep possession of; to avoid losing something.*
    Louise divorced her husband, but she still wanted to _____ his name.

13. *to move from one place to another.*
    In the winter many birds _____ from the cold north to the warm south.

DOWN

1. *a plan for work.*
   Painting an apartment in just one day is an ambitious _____.

3. *to change from one thing to another.*
   When you travel, it is necessary to _____ your money into the currency of the countries you are visiting.

5. *to tell in advance what will happen.*
   The daily horoscope claims to _____ what will happen to you during each day.

6. *to cause someone or something to be active; to excite.*
   An electric current is sometimes used to _____ the brain.

7. *to work together; to agree in timing, manner of doing something, etc.*
   Let's _____ our plans so we can be sure that each one of us is doing the right thing at the right time.

9. *to declare forcefully; to state something with certainty.*
   Because she did not _____ her ideas loudly, no one paid any attention to them.

Checklist 5

In this list, the noun is formed by adding either *-ance* or *-ence* to the verb. The pronunciation of the endings is the same and there are no useful rules to determine which ending is used. In the first group, the noun is spelled with *-ance*.

VERBS	NOUNS	ADJECTIVES	ADVERBS
assist	assistance assistant		
assure	assurance	assured	assuredly
ignore	ignorance	ignorant	ignorantly
inherit disinherit	inheritance heredity heritage	inherited hereditary	
maintain	maintenance		
rely	reliance reliability	(un)reliable	(un)reliably
signify	(in)significance	(in)significant	(in)significantly

In the following group, the noun is spelled with *-ence*.

adhere	adherence adhesion	adherent adhesive	
cohere	(in)coherence cohesion	(in)coherent cohesive	(in)coherently
correspond	correspondence correspondent	corresponding	correspondingly
infer	inference	inferential	
insist	insistence	insistent	insistently
occur	occurrence		
persist	persistence	persistent	persistently
precede	precedence precedent	preceding unprecedented	
transcend	transcendence	transcendent transcendental	

Exercise 5

Each of the following groups of sentences is preceded by a verb. For each sentence in the group, decide on the correct word form — verb, noun, adjective or adverb — and write it on the line at the right.

to inherit

1. When his father dies, the eldest son will _____ all the money.

          ————————

2. The plays of Shakespeare are part of the literary _____ of the English-speaking people.

          ————————

3. Many Indian tribes in the United States are now claiming their _____ rights to their homelands.

          ————————

to persist

4. Ricardo has shown great _____ in his determination to understand vector components in physics.

5. Mary _____ asked her son to clean up his room.

          ————————

6. Billy _____ in asking his parents to let him sleep with his pet frog.

          ————————

to rely

7. Joe puts too much _____ on pills from the drugstore and does not listen to his doctor.

          ————————

8. Mr. Jensen's memory is not very _____. He often forgets the names of his students.

          ————————

9. When Jim's car broke down last week, he had to _____ on his neighbor to give him a ride to work.

          ————————

Select the one word from the four choices that best completes the sentence. Write *the correct form of the word* on the line at the right.

10. We would be wise not to _____ the health warnings printed on each pack of cigarettes.

          ————————

    assure   ignore   adhere   transcend

11. The election of a woman as president of the local plumber's union set a _____ for the future.

          ————————

    signify   precede   persist   rely

12. Olga didn't need any _____ from her father to do her physics homework.

          ————————

    assist   maintain   adhere   insist

13. Everyone must agree to _____ to the plan. Once we begin, there can be no changes at all.

    inference   coherence   adherence   assurance

14. John's actions do not always _____ to his words.

    correspond   adhere   signify   occur

15. Joe was unable to _____ his lead in the race.

    maintain   condense   inherit   assist

16. The pilot _____ Alice that flying is safe.

    precede   assure   persist   retain

17. Ms. Lee told Ken that because his ideas were disorganized, his composition lacked _____.

    transcend   cohere   correspond   adhere

18. Ali put _____ tape over his bandage.

    various   adhesive   coherent   ignorant

19. Uncle Edward _____ the noise of his wife's party and continued to read his newspaper.

    ignorant   coherent   persistent   transcendent

20. Billy's mother became angry and told him to stop shouting or he would _____ her patience.

    transcend   inherit   precede   imply

21. It is a rare _____ when Ms. O'Malley is wrong.

    assist   maintain   infer   occur

Notice the difference in meaning between *infer* and *imply*.

> *To infer* means to arrive at a conclusion by reasoning from facts or evidence: "I infer from your remarks that you think I am a liar."

> *To imply* means to state an idea indirectly, to hint or suggest: "Are you implying that I am not telling the truth?"

> Remember that *I infer* something from what *you imply*.

In the following sentences, use *implied, implication, inferred* and *inference*.

22. Amy's _____ that Joe was stupid didn't bother him at all.

23. From her tone of voice, the students _____ that their teacher was angry with them.

24. Maxine's posture and attitude _____ boredom.

25. Lou's _____ from his boss's criticism was that the boss considered him unfit for the job.

Checklist 6

In the first group of words in this list, the noun is formed by adding *-ment* to the verb.

VERBS	NOUNS	ADJECTIVES	ADVERBS
abandon	abandonment	abandoned	
accompany	accompaniment	accompanying (un)accompanied	
accomplish	accomplishment	accomplished	
achieve	achievement	achievable	
adjust	adjustment	(un)adjustable (un)adjusted	
attain	attainment	(un)attainable	
commit	commitment	(un)committed	
establish	establishment	established	
induce	inducement		
involve	involvement	(un)involved	
obtain	obtainment	(un)obtainable	
reinforce	reinforcement	reinforced	
require	requirement	required	

In the following group of words, the noun is formed by adding *-ption* to a slightly changed form of the verb.

absorb	absorption	absorbent	

assume	assumption	assumed	
conceive	conception concept	(in)conceivable conceptual	(in)conceivably
misconceive	misconception		
perceive	perception	perceivable (im)perceptible perceptive	(im)perceptibly perceptively

Exercise 6

Complete each of the following sentences with an appropriate word form of one of the verbs below. You may use a verb, noun, adjective or adverb form. Note that there are more words than necessary. Use the prefix *un-*, *in-* or *im-* where needed.

abandon	achieve	commit	induce	reinforce
accompany	adjust	conceive	obtain	require

1. Landing on the moon was a great _____, a "giant leap for mankind." _____

2. You must _____ the microscope correctly before you can see through it clearly. _____

3. The storm was so fierce and the ship was leaking so badly that the captain ordered everyone to _____ ship. _____

4. Because the walls of the cathedral were no longer strong, they had to be _____ with steel and stone. _____

5. Ms. Davis will never allow her students to _____ the serious error of confusing *imply* with *infer*. _____

6. Although we have made a lot of progress in space exploration, it is rather _____ that people will be able to live on the moon within the near future. _____

7. Even though Uncle Edward wanted Aunt Emma to _____ him on the fishing trip, she decided not to go. _____

28

8. The chance of a perfect grade on the vocabulary test was a great _____ for Mario to study hard during the weekend. _____

Each of the following groups of sentences is preceded by a verb. For each sentence in the group, decide on the correct word form — verb, noun, adjective or adverb — and write it on the line at the right. Use the prefix *im-* or *in-* where needed.

to perceive

9. Many stars are so far away that they are _____ to the naked eye. They can be seen only through a telescope. _____

10. Our teacher is very _____; she is aware of most of our needs and fears. _____

11. Mrs. Setian's _____ of the world around her is quite different from that of her husband. _____

12. As soon as we entered our principal's home, we _____ that he was a man of excellent taste. _____

to involve

13. The senator's speeches are always so _____ that it is difficult to follow his line of thought. _____

14. The woman's _____ with the criminal was never satisfactorily proved. _____

to conceive

15. Pierre has no real _____ of what a physicist is or does. _____

16. Nowadays, it is difficult for us to _____ of life without electricity. _____

17. It is _____ to think of anyone ever swimming from New York to London. _____

Select the one word from the four choices that best completes the sentence. Write *the correct form of the word* on the line at the right.

18. Susan _____ that it was a very cold day when she looked out the window and saw people wearing heavy coats, hats and gloves. _____

   attain   assume   abandon   obtain

19. This paper towel can _____ more water than that paper towel.

    perceive   obtain   absorb   achieve

    _____

20. While traveling in South America, Nora found that delicious fresh tropical fruits were _____ almost everywhere.

    conceive   attain   perceive   obtain

    _____

21. Billy considered it a great _____ to be able to spell his last name.

    commit   accomplish   involve   induce

    _____

22. The curtain rod is _____. It can be made longer or shorter to fit any window in the house.

    adjust   obtain   absorb   attain

    _____

23. Picasso _____ considerable recognition and success during his lifetime.

    reinforce   attain   assume   absorb

    _____

24. A high school diploma is _____ for entrance into college.

    require   abandon   achieve   accomplish

    _____

25. Victoria and her father _____ the family business in 1961.

    induce   accompany   establish   commit

    _____

Checklist 7

In this list, all the verbs end with *-ize*.

VERBS	NOUNS	ADJECTIVES	ADVERBS
atomize	atom	atomic	
authorize	authority authorization authoritarian author	authoritative (un)authorized authoritarian	authoritatively
categorize	category	categorical	categorically
centralize decentralize	centralization decentralization	central decentralized	centrally
criticize	critic criticism	(un)critical	(un)critically
dramatize	drama dramatization dramatist	(un)dramatic	(un)dramatically
economize	economy economics economist	(un)economic (un)economical	(un)economically
emphasize	emphasis	emphatic	emphatically
hypothesize	hypothesis	hypothetical	hypothetically
individualize	individual individuality individualization	individual	individually
intellectualize	intellectual intellect intelligence intelligibility	(un)intellectual (un)intelligent (un)intelligible	 (un)intelligently
internalize	internalization	internal	internally

legalize	legality	(il)legal	(il)legally
mobilize	mobility	(im)mobile	
neutralize	neutrality	neutral	
normalize	norm normality abnormality	normal abnormal	normally abnormally
philosophize	philosophy philosopher	philosophical	philosophically
polarize	pole polarity polarization	polar	
rationalize	rationality rationale	(ir)rational	(ir)rationally
stabilize	stability instability	stable unstable	
summarize	summary		
symbolize	symbol symbolism	symbolic	symbolically
synthesize	synthetic	synthetic	synthetically
theorize	theory theoretician	theoretical	theoretically
terrorize	terror terrorism terrorist	terrible	terribly
visualize	vision (in)visibility visualization	(in)visible visual	visibly

Exercise 7

Select the one word from the four choices that best completes the sentence. Write *the correct form of the word* on the line at the right.

1. Research has produced many new _____ that will be used in the manufacture of a variety of goods.

   hypotheses   summaries   synthetics   emphases

2. Mr. Maloney couldn't understand his wife's unreasonable desire to eat pickles and ice cream at 2:00 AM. He worried about her _____ demands of this kind.

   irrational   uneconomical   theoretical   internal

3. Because of the development of lightweight, _____ cameras, television reporters can televise news wherever and whenever it is happening.

   visual   mobile   synthetic   abnormal

4. The doctor told the parents that the child's illness had reached a _____ point; the next few hours would determine whether she lived or died.

   criticize   neutralize   polarize   categorize

5. After more than thirty years, the United States and China have begun to _____ their relations.

   economize   normalize   decentralize   polarize

6. Some people miss the emotional insight of poetry when they _____ about the meter, rhyme, symbolism or "messages" of the poem.

   emphasis   category   intellect   rationality

7. The two groups were in total disagreement; in fact, their viewpoints were so _____ that there seemed no chance at all to reach an agreement of any kind.

   atomic   centralized   polarized   stabilized

8. Buying large packages of food is often more _____ than buying small ones.

   economize   authorize   stabilize   intellectualize

9. By repeating "No!" several times, each time a little bit louder, Maria stated her refusal _____.

   visible   synthetic   economical   emphatic

10. Unlike other small children, Cris refused to eat anything during the day and he would eat only bananas and peanut butter at night. His parents could not understand his _____ behavior. _____

affectionate   neutral   abnormal   philosophical

11. Although Ms. Akira pointed out many weak points in Frank's composition, her _____ was generally fair and reasonable. _____

criticize   authorize   individualize   neutralize

12. The architect described the plan for the house, but I had trouble trying to _____ it. _____

stable   normal   categorical   visual

13. Because she enjoys learning about the production and distribution of wealth, Beatriz would like to study _____. _____

philosophy   symbolism   economics   visibility

14. Because of his knowledge and experience, as well as his many successful operations, Dr. Becker is recognized as a well-known _____ in the field of surgical medicine. _____

category   authority   polarity   economist

Complete each of the following sentences with another form of the underlined word.

15. While trying to reach the North Pole, the explorers were threatened by _____ winds. _____

16. The opposite of stability is _____. _____

17. Although my grandfather knows that his fear of ghosts is not rational, he still cannot behave _____ when he hears strange noises in the house. _____

18. Because of his latest dramatic success in Toronto, the Canadian _____ was invited to write a play for the Queen's Silver Jubilee. _____

Each of the following groups of sentences is preceded by a verb. For each sentence in the group, decide on the correct word form—verb, noun, adjective or adverb—and write it on the line at the right.

to emphasize

19. When pronouncing the word *contribute*, many students put the _____ on the wrong syllable.　　　　_____

20. The lecturer said that she wanted to _____ the importance of an idea, so she said it again and again.　　　　_____

21. The teacher's reply to the students was _____: No, she would *not* postpone the test!　　　　_____

22. Gertrude _____ told her boyfriend that she would not discontinue her belly-dancing lessons.　　　　_____

to theorize

23. The professor preferred _____ to practice.　　　　_____

24. The politician's argument was _____ reasonable, but the audience did not agree with his conclusion.　　　　_____

25. Van Hoeschel is considered a great _____ in the field of electrophysiothermodynamics.　　　　_____

Checklist 8

In this and the following list, the verb and the noun have the same form, although there may be other noun forms as well.

VERBS	NOUNS	ADJECTIVES	ADVERBS
aid	aid	(un)aided	
ally	ally alliance	(un)allied	
appeal	appeal	(un)appealing	appealingly
approach	approach	approaching (un)approachable	
avail	avail availability	(un)available	
benefit	benefit benefactor	beneficial	
bomb bombard	bomb bombing bombardment		
collapse	collapse	collapsible	
compound	compound	compound	
conduct	conduct conductor		
conflict	conflict	conflicting	
contact	contact		
contrast	contrast	contrasting contrastive	
design	design		

diagram	diagram		
dispute	dispute	(un)disputed (in)disputable	
feature	feature	featured	
finance	finance financier	financial	financially

Exercise 8

Complete each of the following sentences with an appropriate word form of one of the verbs below. You may use a verb, noun, adjective or adverb form. Note that there are more verbs than necessary.

aid	bombard	diagram
ally	collapse	dispute
appeal	compound	feature
avail	design	finance

1. The enemy's large guns _____ the seaport for several days.

2. Leonard's girlfriend wore a dress with an unusual _____ of yellow flowers and green snakes.

3. The engineer took out a pencil and _____ some ideas on the tablecloth.

4. My grandfather's most obvious facial _____ is his toothless smile.

5. Although the senator _____ to the voters for their support, he lost the election.

6. Mildred never dared to question or _____ her husband's judgment.

7. Salt is a _____ of sodium and chloride.

8. Although my grandmother is becoming deaf, she refuses to wear a hearing _____.

9. New York City is the _____ capital of the United States. The country's most important banks and stock exchanges are located there.

_____

10. Jimmy cried and cried, but his tears were to no _____. His babysitter would not let him eat a seventh ice cream cone.

_____

Complete each of the following sentences with an appropriate word form of one of the verbs below. You may use a verb, noun, adjective or adverb form. Note that there are more verbs than necessary. Use the prefix *un-* or *in-* where needed.

ally	collapse	contact
approach	compound	contrast
avail	conduct	dispute
benefit	conflict	feature

11. Your idea that Columbus discovered America in 1490 _____ with the historical facts.

_____

12. To protect themselves, the two countries agreed to form a military _____.

_____

13. Fresh air and long walks are _____ to your health.

_____

14. Eddie could not _____ the truth; he was the handsomest boy in the class.

_____

15. Professor Schiller will _____ the university orchestra at the annual concert.

_____

16. Electricity flows through the wires when the switch _____ the terminal.

_____

17. Eleanor was unhappy because the store had the dress she wanted in every size but hers, and the dress was _____ at any other store.

_____

18. The _____ of light and shade is important in photography.

_____

19. Unless the wall is reinforced, it will _____.

_____

20. Mr. Martinez was a rather _____ person. He was very distant, and students were afraid to come near him. _____

Complete each of the following sentences with another form of the underlined word.

21. Someone who <u>conducts</u> an orchestra is a _____. _____

22. Someone who deals with <u>finance</u> is a _____. _____

23. Someone who <u>benefits</u> others is a _____. _____

24. Someone whose championship is <u>not disputed</u> is the _____ champion. _____

25. A wooden chair that is easy to carry because it is designed to <u>collapse</u> is a _____ chair. _____

Crossword Puzzle 3

This puzzle contains 15 words from Checklists 5 through 8, plus other words that you probably already know. Solve the puzzle by filling the blanks to complete the sentences.

ACROSS

1. When a ship is sinking, the captain always _____ ship last.
5. Leslie usually stays home in the evenings, but he goes out to a movie now and _____.
8. In the United States it's called a bar. In England it's a _____.
10. I _____ going to solve this puzzle quickly.
12. A _____ is a person who tries to get information secretly.
13. In 1999 New Year's Eve will _____ on a Thursday.
14. I'm going _____ visit my cousin tonight.
15. All living things need _____ in order to survive.
16. In English we say "Take this book from here to there," but "_____ that book from there to here."
18. At the Student-Faculty Association meeting, we will _____ the issue of shorter classes.
20. In order to _____ instruction, the teacher prepared different vocabulary lessons for each student.
22. _____ is the plural ending on such words as *dish* and *watch*.
23. A dictionary is a valuable _____ in learning a new language.
24. An antonym of *hard* is *easy*. Another one is _____.
26. In the United States the weather moves across the country from west to _____.
30. A crowd of people watched in _____ as the burning building collapsed.
32. Orville has a _____ as a night watchman while he studies engineering during the day.
34. Kenneth is _____ fat that he cannot tie his own shoes.
35. *Monsieur* in French _____ to *Mister* or *Sir* in English.
38. Before a test, our teacher always _____ all the important points from our lessons.

DOWN

1. For many people, the _____ of foreign travel is getting to know about other cultures.
2. _____ is the abbreviation for Boston University.

41

3. There is so much to learn about Shakespeare that I cannot _____ it all at once.

4. Mildred told the children to play in the park but not to go too _____ the lake.

6. Jack _____ to go home now because his mother's calling him.

7. The teacher _____ the important words when she speaks in order to help her students understand.

9. External means outside; _____ means the opposite.

11. Whenever Victor _____ a perfect score on his vocabulary test, he shows everyone his paper.

17. Dionysus was the Greek _____ of wine.

19. Fred's parents always _____ that he spend Christmas with them. They will not take no for an answer.

21. Did Henry Ford _____ his motor company in 1903 or 1904?

25. Nancy bought her new dress _____ only $99.95.

27. Before driving, be sure to _____ your rear-view mirror so you can see behind you clearly.

28. _____ is a suffix meaning "the one who" which is added to such verbs as *work* or *paint*.

29. Don't wait too long. Come visit us again _____.

31. A person who learns another language easily is sometimes said to have a good _____ for languages.

33. John should behave himself at parties. Although he's 40, he _____ as if he were 14.

34. *Etc.* is an abbreviation that means "and _____ forth."

36. In the Caribbean, drinks are often made with _____.

37. After he was knighted by the Queen, Churchill became _____ Winston.

Crossword Puzzle 4

Use the following definitions and sentences to solve this crossword puzzle. All the words are from Checklists 5 through 8. Check your answers with the Answer Key.

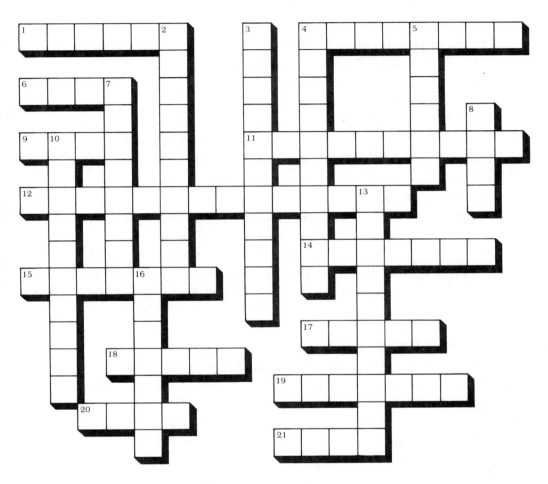

ACROSS

1. *A person skilled in judging books, movies, music, art, plays, etc.*
   The _____ who reviewed Robert Redford's latest film didn't like it at all.

4. *to fall into a disorganized mass.*
   The wooden building is so old that it will soon _____.

6. *help, support.*
   Charts, maps, graphs and diagrams are useful visual _____ in a textbook.

9. *a standard; what is commonly expected.*
An eight-hour day is the _____ in most offices and factories.

11. *to strengthen by adding more supporting material.*
That wooden building will have to be _____.

12. *the successful completion of something.*
Florence Nightengale is famous for her _____ of improving nursing care in hospitals.

14. The adjective form of 13 DOWN.

15. *to be first or ahead of in position, time or importance.*
Does "e" _____ "i" in "receive?"

17. *of use toward a goal or purpose.*
She tried to learn how to cook, but all her efforts were of no _____.

18. *to draw the meaning from something; to conclude*
Looking at the man's old and torn clothing, it is possible to _____ that he is very poor.

19. *capable of being seen.*
The ocean is _____ from my window, but not from yours.

20. *an explosive, often dropped from an airplane.*
Only one _____ landed on the town, but ten people died.

21. *a person or country joined with another for a particular purpose.*
Italy was an important _____ of Germany during World War II.

DOWN

2. *to agree with, or to match.*
In the Celsius scale, does 0° _____ to 32° Fahrenheit?

3. An adjective form of *contrast.*

4. *a promise*
Marriage should be a lifetime _____.

5. *to soak up, like a blotter or paper towel.*
A sponge can _____ a lot of water.

7. *standing for or representing something else.*
On the flag of the United States, the thirteen red and white stripes are _____ of the thirteen original colonies.

8. *to depend on.*
Good friends _____ on one another.

10. *a happening or event.*
Sunrise is a daily _____.

13. *the condition of a country or person that takes no part in a war or argument.*
During World War II, Switzerland maintained its _____.

16. *the management of money and other resources of a nation.*
The discovery of oil in Saudi Arabia changed its whole _____.

Checklist 9

This list is a continuation of Checklist 8, in which the verb and the noun have the same form, although there may be other noun forms as well.

VERBS	NOUNS	ADJECTIVES	ADVERBS
function	function	functional	functionally
grant	grant		
interview	interview interviewer		
issue	issue		
label	label		
labor	labor laborer	laborious	laboriously
orbit	orbit	orbital	
phase in phase out	phase		
plot	plot		
process	process	processed	
range	range		
rebel	rebel rebellion	rebellious	
release	release		
research	research researcher		
shift	shift		

torture	torture	
trace	trace	
transfer	transfer	transferable non-transferable

Exercise 9

Select the one word from the four choices that best completes the sentence. Write *the correct form of the word* on the line at the right.

1. Since the mid-1960s, equal rights for women has been an important political _____ in the United States.

   issue   grant   interview   rebellion   _____

2. After analyzing the dust, scientists found a small but definite _____ of radioactive carbon.

   plot   label   trace   shift   _____

3. The sudden change of policy represented an unexpected _____ in the government's foreign policy.

   transfer   shift   orbit   function   _____

4. Because Hector reads the _____ on everything he buys, he knew that the liquid in the bottle was poisonous.

   plots   labels   traces   shifts   _____

5. Before you can be recommended for the position, a committee must _____ you in order to learn more about you.

   grant   transfer   process   interview   _____

6. John Glenn was the first American astronaut to _____ the earth.

   function   phase   orbit   label   _____

7. The _____ of this movie was based on a poem written in the early twentieth century.

   plot   interview   labor   release   _____

8. The customer thought the chair was attractive but not very _____; it was uncomfortable to sit on and not well constructed.

   transfer   labor   function   orbit

   _____

9. In Hawaii there is very little _____ in temperature.

   trace   range   release   phase

   _____

10. The people _____ against the cruel king and took control of the government.

    process   function   issue   rebel

11. The _____ of making rubber tires for automobiles was developed early in the twentieth century.

    labor   plot   torture   process

    _____

12. Because Ms. Tzechkovitz's secretary never learned to pronounce her name correctly, she _____ her to another office in the company.

    orbit   phase   transfer   plot

13. Many people think that the full story of Hitler's death has not yet been _____.

    range   release   grant   rebel

    _____

14. Doctors and scientists are continuing their _____ into the causes and cures of cancer.

    research   interviews   labors   labels

    _____

15. Jane held onto the dog's tail and wouldn't _____ it, so the dog turned and bit her hand.

    torture   process   release   trace

    _____

Complete each of the following sentences with an appropriate word form of one of the verbs below. You may use a verb, noun, adjective or adverb form. Note that there are more verbs than necessary.

grant	phase	shift
issue	plot	torture
label	process	trace
labor	rebel	transfer

16. The diggers had to work long and _____ in order to finish the hole on schedule.

_____

17. The guards _____ the man all night to force him to reveal his secrets.

_____

18. When Dr. Papadatos was promoted to chief surgeon of the hospital, she entered a new _____ of her medical career.

_____

19. Sometimes during the winter the wind _____ rapidly from one direction to another.

_____

20. The _____ on the cereal box claims "Double your money back if you are not fully satisfied!"

_____

21. Rosa hoped that her government would give her a financial _____ to finish her studies.

_____

22. Limiting nuclear weapons is a serious _____ in the world today.

_____

23. If you can't attend the concert tomorrow, please give your ticket to someone else; it is _____.

_____

24. Government troops are now stationed outside all the major cities in the country in an effort to discourage the _____ tribes.

_____

25. In 1978 the United States government uncovered a secret _____ to steal a nuclear submarine.

_____

Checklist 10

This list includes a miscellaneous group of verbs whose noun, adjective or adverb forms do not follow any particular pattern.

VERBS	NOUNS	ADJECTIVES	ADVERBS
affect	affection affectation	affectionate affected	affectionately
alternate	alternative	alternative alternate	alternatively
analyze	analysis analyst	analytical	analytically
approximate	approximation	approximate	approximately
assemble	assembly	(un)assembled	
coincide	coincidence	coincidental	coincidentally
commune	commune community communism communist	communal communistic	
consist	(in)consistency	(in)consistent	(in)consistently
convene	convention	(un)conventional	(un)conventionally
deny	denial	(un)deniable	undeniably
devise	device		
distinguish	distinction distinctiveness	(in)distinct distinctive (un)distinguished (in)distinguishable	(in)distinctly distinctively
elaborate	elaboration	elaborate	elaborately

encode	code	coded	
decode			
err	error	erroneous	erroneously
horrify	horror	horrible	horribly
		horrid	

Exercise 10

Select the one word from the four choices that best completes the sentence. Write *the correct form of the word* on the line at the right.

1. The very cold weather in Florida seriously _____ the orange crop.   _____

   err   horrify   affect   assemble

2. Mahatma Gandhi was loved by millions of Indians. Their _____ for him was shown by their loving manner and their willingness to follow his beliefs.   _____

   commune   affect   convene   consist

3. The Bensons wanted only a simple home, not a Victorian mansion with so many architectural details and _____ decorations.   _____

   elaborate   analyze   devise   coincide

4. We have to take either the road that goes to the left or the road that goes to the right. There is no other _____.   _____

   deny   alternate   approximate   elaborate

5. It was such a _____ when Pat and Mike met each other in Tokyo. Each thought that the other was still in Hong Kong.   _____

   convene   consist   distinct   coincide

6. Any problem in math is easy if one identifies the facts, studies the steps and looks at the problem

   _____.   _____

   err   consist   deny   analyze

7. You should easily recognize Ms. Sanchez if you see her. She has a very _____ mark on her left cheek.

_____

alternative   coincidental   distinctive   deniable

8. The prisoner first said that he had been at home at the time of the crime. Later he said he had been visiting his girlfriend. _____ statements of this kind made the judge suspect he was not telling the truth.

_____

unconventional   inconsistent   indistinct   unassembled

9. Henry David Thoreau, a nineenth-century American author, lived alone at Walden Pond in order to _____ with nature.

_____

convene   alternate   coincide   commune

10. An American football team _____ of eleven players.

_____

assemble   consist   devise   coincide

11. You cannot desire freedom for yourself and at the same time _____ it to others.

_____

encode   approximate   deny   affect

12. A mousetrap is a useful _____ that catches and kills mice.

_____

deny   devise   encode   decode

13. Although it was getting dark, the hunters could still _____ the difference between a bear and another hunter.

_____

assemble   distinguish   elaborate   convene

14. Dr. Perry _____ the blood sample and found a low level of iron.

_____

decode   approximate   consist   analyze

15. Names of cities, countries and languages are _____ capitalized in English.

_____

erroneous   conventional   distinct   elaborate

16. *Pi* is _____ equal to $\frac{22}{7}$ or 3.14.

_____

horrible   approximate   distinctive   communal

17. Henry Ford was an industrial pioneer who invented a fast method for the _____ of automobiles which is still used today.

    community   consistent   assembly   affectionate

18. Dwight tries to impress people by using French words in his speech. However, most people are more irritated than impressed by that _____.

    alternative   affectation   coincidence   elaboration

19. A system of telegraphic dots and dashes was a _____ which Samuel Morse developed for international communication.

    horror   device   code   distinction

20. Many students have the _____ belief that British English is somehow more pure and perfect than American English.

    communistic   alternate   erroneous   indistinct

21. Paul's teacher reacted with _____ at the many four-letter words in his composition.

    affection   horror   coincidence   analysis

22. The chemist's original _____ of the compound was incorrect.

    analyze   approximate   consist   devise

23. Although Margaret tried to _____ the fact, all her friends were sure that she dyed her gray hair red.

    encode   deny   assemble   convene

24. Willie's mother was certain that he had been smoking because there was a very _____ smell of cigarette smoke in his room.

    deniable   affected   communal   distinct

25. J. Thomas Mountebank hoped to _____ a little gadget that would make his car get over 100 miles per gallon of gas.

    analyze   convene   devise   decode

Checklist 11

This list is a continuation of Checklist 10.

VERBS	NOUNS	ADJECTIVES	ADVERBS
impel	impulse	impulsive	impulsively
inhabit	habitation inhabitant	habitable (un)inhabitable	
intensify	intensity	intense intensive	intensely intensively
invert	inversion inverse	inverse	inversely
liberate liberalize	liberation liberal liberator liberalization	liberal	liberally
major (in)	major majority	major	
prevail	prevalence	prevalent	
proceed	procedure proceedings proceeds	procedural	
prosper	prosperity	prosperous	prosperously
publish publicize	publication publisher publicity	(un)published (un)publicized	
respond	response	(un)responsive	
secure	(in)security	(in)secure	(in)securely
succeed	success	(un)successful	(un)successfully

	succession successor	successive	successively
suffice	sufficiency	(in)sufficient	(in)sufficiently
testify	testimony	testimonial	
unify	(dis)unity (dis)unification uniformity uniform	(dis)united (dis)unified (un)uniform	uniformly
vacate	vacancy	vacant	
validate	validity	(in)valid	

Exercise 11

Select the one word from the four choices that best completes the sentence. Write *the correct form of the word* on the line at the right.

1. People in prehistoric times often _____ caves. _____

   unify   publicize   inhabit   invert

2. The oil industry has brought great _____ to Saudi Arabia. _____

   proceed   prosper   suffice   unify

3. If you want to take more than five courses in one term, you must first _____ permission from the Student Request Committee. _____

   secure   prevail   inhabit   liberate

4. Although the professor questioned the _____ of the student's excuse, she allowed him to take a make-up exam. _____

   intense   publicize   secure   validate

5. Be sure to keep the chemicals at a _____ temperature; the heat should not vary at all. _____

   procedure   unify   major   testify

6. Because his driving test is next week, Mark has to _____ his effort to learn how to park in small spaces.   _____

   invert   proceed   intensify   testify

7. In World War II the Allies suffered a long _____ of defeats before they finally achieved victory.   _____

   succeed   prosper   publicize   unify

8. In order to impress his friends, Ron always leaves a very _____ tip for the waitress at Pasquale's Restaurant.   _____

   vacant   liberal   testimonial   prosperous

9. Young children appreciate being loved, and they are very _____ to affection.   _____

   impel   intensify   respond   prevail

10. The supply of gasoline is in _____ relationship to its price. As the supply goes down, the price goes up.   _____

    inverse   intense   insecure   insufficient

11. I need to move to a larger apartment. Do you know of any _____ ones in this neighborhood?   _____

    validate   vacate   succeed   major

12. Figuring out one's income tax can be a difficult and tiring _____.   _____

    testimony   impulse   procedure   succession

13. In order to appeal to a wider group of voters, the candidate is starting to _____ her views on certain issues.   _____

    invert   liberalize   impel   vacate

Each of the following groups of sentences is preceded by a verb. For each sentence in the group, decide on the correct word form — verb, noun, adjective or adverb — and write it on the line at the right. Use the prefix *un-* or *in-* where needed.

to inhabit

14. After the fire, the guest room was _____ because of the smoke and water.   _____

15. An _____ of the island of Malta is called a Maltese.

_____

to prevail

16. A belief in magic still _____ among some tribes in the jungles of Brazil.

_____

17. The _____ of glaucoma and other eye diseases is a serious concern in the Middle East.

_____

18. Typhoid is no longer _____ anywhere in the world.

_____

to suffice

19. A dozen hot dogs should be a _____ number for three Boy Scouts.

_____

20. Because my teacher felt that my knowledge of early Egyptian architecture was _____, I received a failing grade in the course.

21. Mr. Ricciardi wanted a 25% raise in pay, but after talking to his boss, he decided that a 5% raise would have to _____.

_____

Complete each of the following sentences with another form of the underlined word.

22. A sudden _____ of anger <u>impelled</u> Gino to throw the alarm clock out of the window.

_____

23. The movie star's romance was so well <u>publicized</u> that a little more _____ did not seem to matter.

_____

24. A <u>major</u> problem in some democracies is to get a _____ of the people to vote.

_____

25. The blind man wanted to <u>testify</u> that the thief had blue eyes and blond hair, but the judge would not accept his _____.

_____

Checklist 12

None of the remaining lists contain any verbs. The adjective and adverb forms are related to each noun in a variety of ways.

VERBS	NOUNS	ADJECTIVES	ADVERBS
	(in)accuracy	(in)accurate	(in)accurately
	adult adulthood	adult	
	aggression aggressiveness aggressor	aggressive	aggressively
	analogy	analogical analogous	analogically analogously
	anecdote	anecdotal	
	(in)appropriateness	(in)appropriate	(in)appropriately
	atmosphere	atmospheric	
	biology biologist	biological	biologically
	(in)capability	(in)capable	capably
	chemical chemistry chemist	chemical	chemically
	circumstance	circumstantial	
	classic classics	classic classical	
	complexity complex	complex	

consequence	consequent (in)consequential	consequently
(in)constancy	(in)constant	constantly
contagion	contagious	
contrary	contrary	
(in)credibility (in)credulity	(in)credible (in)credulous	(in)credibly (in)credulously
crisis	(un)critical	(un)critically
culture	cultural cultured	culturally
delinquency delinquent	delinquent	
density	dense	densely
(in)efficiency	(in)efficient	(in)efficiently
element	elementary	
emotion	(un)emotional	(un)emotionally

Exercise 12

Select the one word from the four choices that best completes the sentence. Write *the correct form of the word* on the line at the right.

1. The bank manager congratulated Maria for the
   _____ with which she recorded the transactions
   that she handled.   _____

   anecdotal   accurate   contagious   delinquent

2. _____ to his expectations, Charles managed to
   pass his English test.   _____

   contrary   circumstantial   elementary   appropriate

3. Economists still argue whether the financial
   _____ on Wall Street in 1929 was the cause or

the result of the economic situation throughout the world.   _____

constancy   efficiency   element   crisis

4. During the chemical fire, the _____ of the smoke in the area limited visibility.   _____

contagious   emotional   dense   accurate

5. It is difficult for some teen-agers to learn that they have to be willing to accept the _____ of their actions.   _____

atmospheres   credibilities   consequences   delinquencies

6. Adults look back at their childhood with great pleasure, and children always look forward to their _____.   _____

adulthood   analogy   atmosphere   aggression

7. To say that a soldier fought in battle like a lion may be a descriptive _____, but it does not mean that he was on all fours, roaring and wagging his tail!   _____

anecdote   analogy   capability   emotion

8. Loretta's fifteen-year-old son could not understand why it was _____ to wear a sport shirt, blue jeans and sneakers to a formal wedding.   _____

incredulous   inefficient   inappropriate   incapable

9. The police had only _____ evidence in their case against the prisoner. There were no specific clues or definite proof of her guilt.   _____

accuracy   classic   circumstance   delinquency

10. Day after day Martha complained about her husband's cooking. He soon grew tired of her _____ complaints.   _____

analogy   biology   contagion   constancy

11. The police feel that the increasing problem of juvenile _____ is as much a responsibility of the parents as it is of the police.   _____

circumstance   consequence   delinquency   density

12. Bill is so unmechanical and _____ that it took him more than an hour to change a spark plug in his car. _____

    inefficient   unemotional   incredulous   unaggressive

13. When Benjamin caught a _____ disease, none of his friends were allowed to visit him. _____

    consequent   contagious   capable   cultural

14. Aunt Bessie enjoys telling _____ about her romance with Uncle Oscar before they were married —fifty-four years ago. _____

    adulthood   atmospheres   aggressions   anecdotes

15. Ricardo is _____ of doing good work in class when he wants to. His problem is that he seldom wants to. _____

    capability   contrary   element   analogy

16. The United Nations could not agree on which country was guilty of committing the first act of _____. _____

    credibility   aggression   density   accuracy

17. The problem of controlling inflation is more _____ than most people realize. _____

    anecdotal   complex   constant   chemical

18. One _____ of Ruth's refusal to eat her roommate's cooking was a very welcome loss of weight. _____

    appropriateness   consequence   atmosphere   complexity

19. A _____ of insecurity spread among the inhabitants of the village after five houses were robbed. _____

    contagion   analogy   aggression   density

20. Don't judge my little girl until you know the _____ that caused her to kick the cat. _____

    incredibility   classics   contagion   circumstances

Note the possible confusion between *incredible* and *incredulous*:

incredible refers to something (less often, someone) that is unbelievable. It is the negative of *credible*, "capable of being believed."

incredulous refers to someone who does not believe something; it means "unbelieving."

Remember that something incred*ible* is something you are not *able* to believe. *You* are incred*ulous*. For example: John's wife was incredulous when he gave her an incredible explanation of why he was returning home at 3:00 A.M. (The story was unbelievable; therefore, she was unbelieving.)

For each of the following sentences, use one of these words:

credible   credibility   incredible

incredulity   incredulously

21. It is _____ that you should think I would lie.   _____

22. After my long explanation, she looked at me

_____.   _____

23. Why do you doubt what I say? Your _____ amazes me.   _____

24. When the president did not keep his campaign promises, his _____ was seriously questioned.   _____

25. Your story is barely _____, but I have no choice other than to believe it now.   _____

Crossword Puzzle 5

This puzzle contains 20 words from Checklists 9 through 12, plus other words that you probably already know. Solve the puzzle by filling in the blanks to complete the sentences.

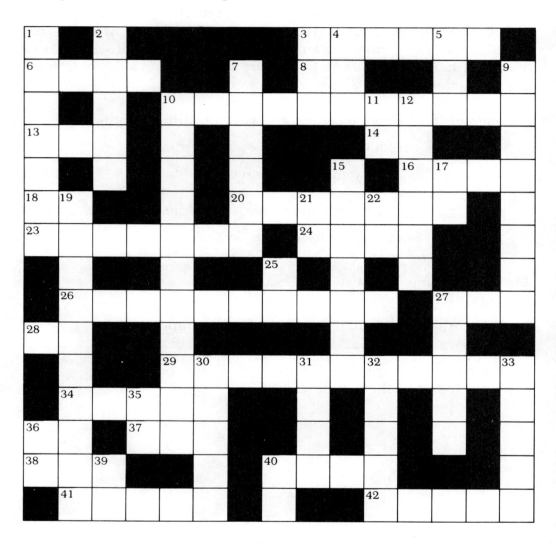

ACROSS

3. That factory has three work _____: from 8:00 to 4:00, from 4:00 to midnight, and from midnight to 8:00.

6. No one can _____ the importance of the automobile in modern life.

8. _____ is an informal greeting.

10. When Alex feels quarrelsome and wants to fight, he takes out his _____ on his cat.

13. I was in the kitchen stirring a _____ of soup when the phone rang.

14. The show begins at 8:30. Please try to arrive _____ time.

16. What _____ do you usually wake up in the morning?

18. A common past tense ending is _____.

20. My brother works for the Department of Defense. The secret messages that he _____ are used in international communications.

23. All the guests are expected to _____ to the invitation by the end of the month.

24. At the end of the prayer, everyone said _____.

26. Valerie's version of what had happened was so _____ that nobody believed it.

27. An informal word for *boy* or *man* is _____.

28. _____ is a prefix that means "not."

29. Ethel was not sure of the exact cost of the new car; she could only remember an _____ price.

34. The American colonists decided to _____ their forces against King George III.

36. A prefix meaning "again" is _____.

37. The English are known for drinking _____.

38. Gilbert tried to pass the government examination several times, and in the _____ he succeeded.

40. The next town isn't very far. It's a _____ two miles down this road.

41. The Washburns can _____ their family name back to twelfth-century England.

42. Some people prefer manual _____ to doing desk work.

DOWN

1. Frank wanted to plug both his television and phonograph into a single electrical outlet, but he didn't have an _____.

2. A well-organized paragraph should have _____ and coherence.

3. _____ hopes to be a mother someday.

4. Jimmy likes _____ father very much.

5. My grandfather loves to go to discos and my grandmother does _____.

7. Agnes likes her teacher, so when he asked her to help him plan the class party, she _____.

9. Students gather in the school auditorium every morning at 8:30 for an _____.

10. It is certainly not _____ to wear a bathing suit to a funeral.

11. Gus broke his leg _____ he couldn't play in the football game.

12. What do you _____ to study when you go to college?

15. A computer is more _____ than a pocket calculator.

17. This puzzle _____ easier than the next one.

19. Arnold was more than just disobedient. He was close to being a juvenile _____.

21. The post office abbreviation for *California* is _____.

22. _____ is a prefix which reverses the meaning of many verbs.

25. A Spanish speaker says *yes* by saying _____.

27. The university gave Dr. Amadeus a research _____ to study the homing instincts of pigeons.

30. The primary purpose of the United Nations is to promote and maintain _____ throughout the world.

31. Why do most fairy tales begin with "_____ upon a time . . ."?

32. The hope of good grades can _____ students to work hard in school.

33. _____ is the noun form of the verb *to err*.

35. "_____ is a nice day" means "the day is nice."

36. Same as 36 ACROSS.

39. The abbreviation for *doctor* is _____.

40. Would you please do _____ a favor?

Crossword Puzzle 6

Use the following definitions and sentences to solve this crossword puzzle. All the words are from Checklists 9 through 12.

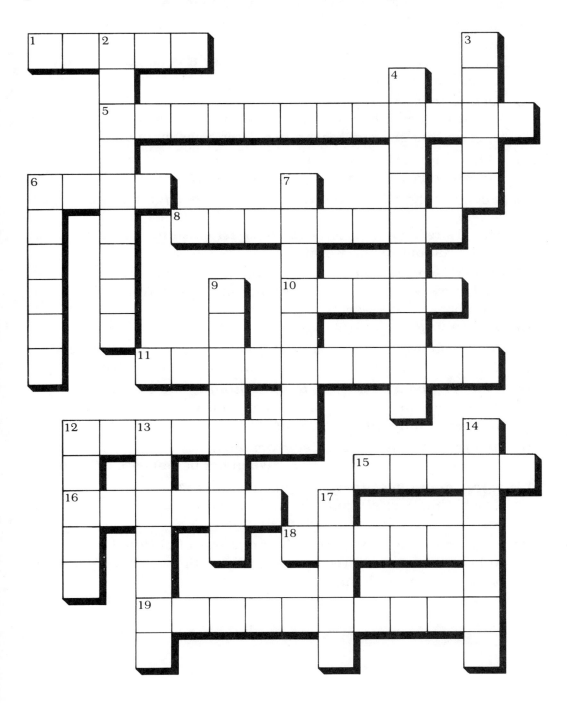

ACROSS

1. *to form into one.*
   Once independence was declared, Washington tried to _____ the military forces of the colonies into a single army.

5. *capable of being moved from one place to another, or of being used by someone or something else.*
   This ticket is issued to you only. Because it is not _____, it cannot be used by anyone else.

6. *declare to be untrue.*
   Because Rachel believed in always being honest, she could not _____ that she had broken her sister's new camera.

8. *a short story, usually amusing, personal or biographical.*
   Vincent told a funny _____ about his vacation in Stockholm.

10. *a combination into one; a joining together for a common purpose.*
    The United Nations is devoted to establishing _____ among all the nations of the world.

11. *able to be passed on by touch; causing much illness.*
    As far as we know, cancer cannot be caught from others; it is not a _____ disease.

12. *opposite in order or position.*
    When you drink a lot of alcohol, your ability to control yourself is in _____ proportion to the amount of alcohol you drink.

15. *a piece of paper attached to something to show what it is.*
    If you read the _____ on the can, you will be surprised by the number of different ingredients.

16. *safe from danger; protected from harm.*
    Jane always feels very _____ when her parents are close to her.

18. *moves or changes from one place to another.*
    Rosalie has had six jobs in the last year. She _____ from one position to another every other month.

19. *keeping to the same principles or course of action.*
    At least the senator's record was _____. She voted against every proposal that would have lowered taxes.

DOWN

2. *the quality of being very strong or great.*
   The _____ of the heat in the desert is sometimes almost un-bearable.

3. *correct or effective, according to formalities or the law.*
   In order to travel outside of your country, you must have a _____ passport.

4. *the occupation of a place.*
   Some prison camps during the war were not fit for human _____.

6. *a small tool or instrument, a gadget, used for a special purpose.*
   Yuri hoped to invent a _____ to tie neckties automatically.

7. *careful and exact.*
   In order not to make any mistakes, a bookkeeper must be very _____ in simple arithmetic.

9. *opposite; not agreeing with.*
   Betty's opinion of Elvis Presley was _____ to that of her parents. They admired him, but she thought he was overrated.

12. *a matter of current interest or discussion.*
   The energy crisis was an important _____ during the political campaigns of the 1970s.

13. *a job or position that is open; a room or an apartment that is for rent.*
   As soon as a _____ occurred in my building, I told my friends who had been looking for an apartment for more than a year.

14. *state of being crowded or close together.*
   The population _____ in Canada is only 5.6 persons per square mile.

17. *a stage of development.*
   The interval between the world wars was the most productive _____ of Maugham's career as a playwright.

Checklist 13

This list is a continuation of Checklist 12. There are no verbs. The adjective and adverb forms are related to each noun in a variety of ways.

VERBS	NOUNS	ADJECTIVES	ADVERBS
	empiricism	empirical	empirically
	energy	energetic	energetically
	environment	environmental	environmentally
	evidence	evident	evidently
	finality	final	finally
	fragment fragmentation	fragmentary	
	graph graphics	graphic	graphically
	gravity gravitation	gravitational	
	heresy heretic	heretical	
	hostility	hostile	
	imperialism imperialist	imperial imperialistic	
	instinct	instinctive	instinctively
	logic logician	(il)logical	(il)logically
	magnitude magnificence	magnificent	magnificently

magic magician	magical	magically
method methodology	methodical methodological	methodically methodologically
metropolis	metropolitan	
military	military militant	militarily
minor minority	minor	
miracle	miraculous	miraculously
notion	notional	
objectivity objective object	(un)objective	objectively
period periodical	periodic periodical	periodically
personality	(im)personal	(im)personally
phenomenon	phenomenal	phenomenally
physiology physiologist physician physique	physical physiological	physically physiologically
(im)precision	(im)precise	(im)precisely
region	regional	regionally
(dis)similarity	(dis)similar	(dis)similarly

Exercise 13

Select the one word from the four choices that best completes the sentence. Write *the correct form of the word* on the line at the right.

1. Abdul is very organized in his study habits. He schedules his time carefully and everything is neatly arranged on his desk. Other students admire his _____ preparation for study. _____

   empirical   methodological   methodical   militant

2. The body has a regular _____ need for sufficient food and occasional rest. _____

   imperialism   notion   physiology   phenomenon

3. Among the broken shells on the beach, Jennifer found a small _____ of a beautiful seashell. _____

   instinct   minority   finality   fragment

4. There are many _____ factors which affect the forests in the mountains and the soil in the plains. _____

   gravity   environment   precision   hostility

5. The child seemed to know _____ that the angry dog was dangerous. _____

   magnificence   energy   instinct   fragment

6. When his mother-in-law visits for longer than a day, John tends to become somewhat cold and _____ towards her. _____

   evident   impersonal   periodical   methodical

7. The church criticized the priest for questioning the validity of the Bible and for his other _____ beliefs. _____

   heresy   military   notion   imperialism

8. The socialist group claimed that several nations had united into an _____ plot to suppress their territorial rights. _____

   imperialistic   environmental   energetic   instinctive

9. Gretchen suffered from _____ headaches that seemed to come and go every two or three weeks. _____

   magic   phenomenon   period   similarity

10. The rooster Chanticleer noticed that the sun rose every time he crowed in the morning. Due to mis-

taken _____, he assumed that his crowing caused the sun to rise.

precision   personality   logic   hostility

_____

11. Tom feels most _____ early in the morning. That's when he likes to run around the park for half an hour.

method   miracle   gravity   energy

_____

12. An eclipse of the sun or moon is a fascinating natural _____ to watch.

environment   phenomenon   magnitude   similarity

_____

13. After a great deal of research, the psychologist finally produced _____ evidence to support her theories about human behavior.

periodical   imprecise   empirical   gravitational

_____

14. Because Helen is his wife, it is difficult for Alan to be _____ about her talent.

objective   fragmentary   heretical   metropolitan

_____

Complete each of the following sentences with another form of the underlined word.

15. The scientist's method of analysis was slow, thorough and unusually _____.

_____

16. The jury was evidently willing to overlook the _____ of lipstick stains on the victim's sleeve.

_____

17. The top tennis stars of Canada and the United States finally met in the _____ championship match of the season.

_____

18. Carlos has such a pleasant personality that it is not surprising that he has so many close _____ friends.

_____

19. Hazel inferred some kind of hostility in her husband's voice, but she couldn't understand why he should be so _____.

_____

Each of the following groups of sentences is preceded by a word. For each sentence in the group, decide on the correct word form—noun, adjective or adverb—and write it on the line at the right.

a miracle

20. Pauline _____ escaped death in a horrible automobile accident.

    _____

21. As soon as Ann's father-in-law left, she made a _____ recovery from her headache.

    _____

22. Miracle Motion Pictures has the motto: "If the movie is good, it's a _____!"

    _____

precision

23. Because the word *nice* has so many different meanings, try to use a more _____ word in your composition.

    _____

24. The wristwatch was made with such _____ that it did not lose more than one second a week.

    _____

25. Mr. Maurizzi met his wife at the tennis courts _____ at 3:25 in the afternoon.

    _____

Checklist 14

This list is a continuation of Checklist 13. There are no verbs. The adjective and adverb forms are related to each noun in a variety of ways.

VERBS	NOUNS	ADJECTIVES	ADVERBS
	portion (dis)proportion	(dis)proportional (dis)proportionate	
	potential	potential (im)potent	potentially
	prime	prime primary primitive	primarily
	province	provincial	
	psychology psychologist	psychological	psychologically
	radical	radical	radically
	(ir)responsibility	(ir)responsible	(ir)responsibly
	section	sectional	
	series	serial	serially
	sex sexuality sexism/sexist	sexual	sexually
	sphere	spherical	
	spontaneity	spontaneous	spontaneously
	structure	structural	structurally

style	stylistic	stylistically
	stylish	stylishly
subject		
subjectivity	subjective	subjectively
substance	substantial	substantially
subtlety	subtle	subtly
suicide	suicidal	
superiority	superior	
technique	technical	technically
technology	technological	technologically
technician		
technicality		
territory	territorial	
tone	tonal	
topic	topical	
tradition	traditional	traditionally
urbanization	urban	
suburb	suburban	
vastness	vast	vastly

Exercise 14

Select the one word from the four choices that best completes the sentence. Write *the correct form of the word* on the line at the right.

1. In this recipe, the flour, sugar and water should be mixed in equal _____. _____

   spontaneity   proportion   potential   superiority

2. Scientists must not allow _____ feelings to influence their research. _____

   subject   substance   province   tradition

3. The prime minister has the most _____ of all elected officials in the British government.

   sphere   style   prime   responsibility

   _____

4. Nothing Helen says is ever _____. She always thinks carefully before she speaks.

   topical   territorial   spontaneous   primary

   _____

5. The opposition party demanded many _____ alterations in their government's foreign policy.

   series   radical   sex   suburb

   _____

6. Although Mr. Hamilton complains about headaches, backaches and stomachaches, his wife argues that his problems are more _____ than physiological.

   psychology   substance   technology   province

   _____

7. Priscilla doesn't like to live in the country. She prefers _____ life.

   subtle   potent   topical   urban

   _____

8. Many people persist in believing that Francis Bacon wrote the plays of Shakespeare, but the _____ of the two authors are quite dissimilar.

   potentials   portions   styles   substances

   _____

9. Mark ate a _____ breakfast of cereal, bacon and eggs, fried potatoes, toast, jelly and five cups of coffee.

   subjective   substantial   suicidal   sectional

   _____

10. Although the secretary had many responsibilities in the office, his _____ responsibility was to type letters for the department head.

    spontaneous   suburban   primary   radical

    _____

11. The taste of oregano was so _____ that it was hardly noticeable.

    superiority   prime   topic   subtlety

    _____

12. Alex is a natural swimmer with strong arms and legs, good coordination and excellent breath con-

trol. It's a shame that he has wasted his _____ by not practicing regularly.

subtlety   portion   potential   tonality

_____

13. The _____ of birds can often be determined by their size, shape and especially by the color of their feathers.

sex   prime   style   urbanization

_____

14. In the mid-nineteenth century, pioneers opened up the western _____ of the United States.

proportion   territory   suburb   substance

_____

15. Jean enjoys riding her motorcycle, but she doesn't much care for the _____ details, such as repairing and maintaining it.

substance   province   technique   structure

_____

16. Roberta inferred from her boyfriend's _____ of voice that he was very angry with her.

spherical   provincial   tonal   topical

_____

17. Felix didn't like the composition _____ which his teacher assigned. He wanted to write about his trip to Europe last summer.

topic   structure   series   spontaneity

_____

18. Brenda told her husband that there is a _____ difference between saying her hat is "awful pretty" and "pretty awful!"

subtle   spontaneous   vast   topical

_____

19. Rosemary felt that her low salary was _____ to her high level of skill.

disproportionate   responsible   traditional   radical

_____

20. An attempt to liberate the prisoners from the heavily guarded camp was practically a _____ act, but a few brave soldiers successfully completed the task.

prime   suicide   style   subtlety

_____

76

21. Americans _____ celebrate Independence Day with fireworks and, perhaps, a picnic.

    spontaneous   subjective   territorial   traditional

22. Before Julius Caesar became dictator of the Roman Empire, he was governor of the _____ of Gaul.

    proportion   province   technique   suburb

23. _____ tools were made from animal bones or sharpened stones.

    provincial   primitive   potential   proportional

24. Dr. Prendergast considers himself _____ to others simply because he has a higher education and earns more money.

    superior   substantial   vaster   primary

25. During the national strike of truck drivers, the government seemed _____ to do anything to settle the dispute.

    radical   subtle   impotent   substantial

Checklist 15

In this list there are only nouns. These nouns have no other common forms.

VERBS	NOUNS	ADJECTIVES	ADVERBS
	area		
	attitude		
	axis (pl. = axes)		
	currency		
	datum (pl. = data)		
	doctrine		
	equilibrium		
	factor		
	instance		
	interval		
	momentum		
	monarch monarchy		
	morale		
	perspective		
	principle		
	ratio		
	source		
	spectrum		

status	
stereotype	
trait	
trend	
version	

Exercise 15

Select the one word from the four choices that best completes the sentence. Write *the correct form of the word* on the line at the right.

1. When his wife didn't have supper ready by the usual time, Mr. Mendoza demonstrated an incredibly childish _____.

   subtlety   status   attitude   currency

   _____

2. Smoking seems to be one of the most important _____ in the increasing number of deaths from cancer.

   factors   intervals   trends   ratios

   _____

3. Although Robert used to be president of the local music club, he no longer has any official _____ with the organization.

   gravity   phenomenon   attitude   status

   _____

4. "Do unto others as you would have them do unto you" is an excellent _____ to live by.

   version   principle   spectrum   momentum

   _____

5. For our term papers, we have to list in footnotes the various _____ we consulted for our information.

   hostility   axis   perspective   source

   _____

6. Shirley was carried forward by the _____ of a high wave and thrown up onto the beach.

   momentum   morale   tradition   trend

   _____

7. When the American colonists proclaimed their independence, they voted to govern themselves by a presidency rather than a _____.

principle   monarchy   stereotype   heresy

_____

8. Because the _____ between the first speech and the second was much too long, the audience became restless.

instinct   interval   similarity   status

_____

9. The current _____ in medical science is for doctors to specialize.

equilibrium   trend   spectrum   version

_____

10. Any candidate for public office tries to satisfy a wide range of voters: old, young, rich, poor, black, white, Republican, Democrat, liberal, conservative – the whole _____ of political opinion.

spectrum   fragmentation   environment   doctrine

_____

11. Edna Jones is a very bad cook; for _____, she cannot even boil water without burning the pot!

instinct   interval   instance   momentum

_____

12. The study of the mysterious "black holes in space" is a new _____ of research in astrophysics.

doctrine   factor   area   morale

_____

13. The _____ of the Divine Right of Kings derived from the Middle Age concept of God's authority on earth.

region   doctrine   status   technology

_____

14. Grandpa Gray perfectly fits the _____ of a lovable old grandfather: he is warm, friendly and full of anecdotes about the past.

spectrum   environment   datum   stereotype

_____

15. When their car broke down in a snowstorm, Suzanne kept up her husband's _____ by singing, joking and assuring him that help would come soon.

heresy   morale   equilibrium   version

_____

Complete each of the following sentences with one of the nouns below. Note that there are more nouns than necessary.

axis	instance	ratio
currency	momentum	status
data	monarch	trait
equilibrium	perspective	version

16. The _____ in the United States and Canada is based on the dollar, while in England it is based on the pound sterling.

17. John and his grandfather look at the world from a totally different _____.

18. The _____ for baldness is transmitted genetically from parents to children.

19. The earth rotates on its _____ every twenty-four hours.

20. The _____ of 100 to 10 is the same as 10 to 1.

21. There are still instruments on the moon that gather scientific _____.

22. I had no difficulty understanding Beckett's play, *En Attendant Godot*, because I had already read the English _____.

23. Once the wagon gained _____, it rolled easily along the track.

24. The _____ of doctors and engineers is usually higher than that of teachers in most countries.

25. Earl was balancing himself on top of the fence when he lost his _____ and fell off.

Checklist 16

In this list there are only adjectives and a related adverb form, if any.

VERBS	NOUNS	ADJECTIVES	ADVERBS
		acute	acutely
		divine	divinely
		domestic	domestically
		ethnic	ethnically
		external	externally
		imperative	
		instant	instantly
		(il)legal	(il)legally
		negative	negatively
		obvious	obviously
		odd	oddly
		positive	positively
		previous	previously
		rural	
		supreme	supremely
		tiny	
		ultimate	ultimately
		virtual	virtually

Exercise 16

Select the one word from the four choices that best completes the sentence. Write *the correct form of the word* on the line at the right.

1. Because one boxer was over 6 feet tall and weighed 230 pounds and the other was only 5 feet 7 inches tall and weighed 175 pounds, it was _____ who would win the fight.

   imperative   obvious   ethnic   ultimate

   _____

2. Three dogs, four cats, a dozen fish and two birds in a cage made the Pandicos' house a _____ zoo.

   virtual   previous   primary   positive

   _____

3. When Suzanne got married, she expected happiness to come _____, but it did not. It took several years and many arguments before she and her husband were truly happy.

   hostile   external   instant   radical

   _____

4. Joseph was disappointed when he got back his vocabulary test. He had been _____ that he would get all the words right.

   positive   evident   imperative   potential

   _____

5. Because he couldn't read, the little boy drank the medicine which was intended for _____ use only.

   ethnic   tiny   imperial   external

   _____

6. Each group in the International Folk Dance Club gave a demonstration of their _____ music and dances.

   instinctive   ethnic   periodic   obvious

   _____

7. Because the operation was scheduled for 7:00, it was _____ for Dr. Wen to be at the hospital by 6:30.

   imperative   ultimate   obvious   similar

   _____

8. The audience reacted very _____ to the unconventional plot and ambiguous conclusion of the play.

    previous   supreme   legal   negative

    _____

9. Lucille enjoyed neither urban nor suburban life. She much preferred to live in a small _____ town.

    domestic   rural   ultimate   ethnic

    _____

10. Igor could sense that something _____ had happened because of the tense atmosphere in the usually relaxed office.

    supreme   environmental   tiny   odd

    _____

11. Dogs have such an _____ sense of smell that they can track a person after several days.

    ultimate   acute   ethnic   external

    _____

12. The employment office asked Bruce to list all the jobs he had before and to give the names of his _____ employers.

    previous   negative   positive   instant

    _____

13. Anita prefers foreign wine to that produced _____.

    divine   obvious   domestic   virtual

    _____

14. Because Mr. MacDonald's car was parked _____, he was given a parking ticket.

    previous   illegal   positive   imperative

    _____

15. The insect was so _____ that Bernice could hardly see it.

    rural   obvious   acute   tiny

    _____

Complete each of the following sentences with an appropriate form of one of the words below. Note that there are more words than necessary.

acute	instant	rural
divine	legal	supreme
domestic	negative	ultimate
imperative	previous	virtual

16. Dwight Eisenhower was the _____ commander of the Allied Forces in Europe during World War II. _____

17. In the United States, some laws differ from state to state. For example, the _____ drinking age varies from 18 to 21. _____

18. While he was disco dancing, Floyd suffered a sudden _____ pain in his back. _____

19. The former movie star had not worked for many years. He was therefore _____ unknown to the younger generation. _____

20. The president may ask advice from many different advisors, but he is _____ responsible for the final decision. _____

21. George's _____ reaction to the war movie was probably due to the fact that he detests violence. _____

22. Mario tried to repair the television even though he had never done it before and had no _____ experience with electricity or electronics. _____

23. The priest prayed for _____ guidance. _____

24. Public opinion polls indicate that people feel the president is more effective in his foreign policy than in _____ affairs. _____

25. When Ms. Williams asked Tim to spell *occurred*, he stood up and spelled it _____ without any hesitation. _____

Crossword Puzzle 7

This puzzle contains 15 words from Checklists 13 through 16, plus other words that you probably already know. Solve the puzzle by filling in the blanks to complete the sentences.

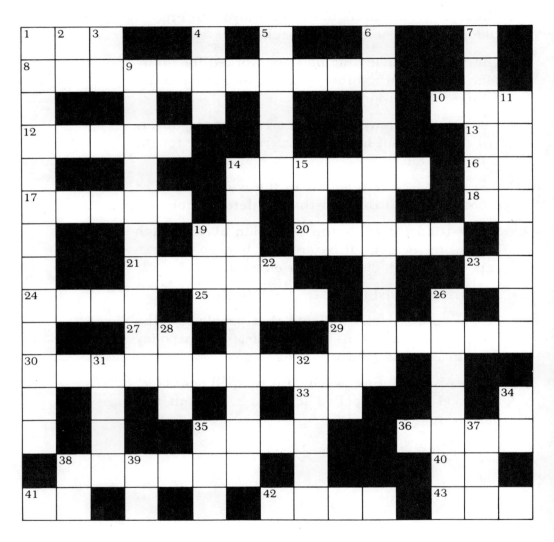

ACROSS

1. _____ likes to wear her hair long.
8. There are many ways of looking at this problem, so let's try to keep it in its proper _____.
10. 2, 4, 6 and 8 are even numbers; 1, 3, 5 and 7 are _____.

12. The opposite of *always* is _____.
13. Although I tried to _____ my best, I failed the exam.
14. Sandra likes her English teacher's _____ of teaching.
16. Emily Martin's initials are _____.
17. Some people serve salad before the main course at dinner; others serve it _____.
18. _____ is a prefix that means "again."
19. The automobile accident occurred _____ the corner of Main Street and Fulton Avenue.
20. Generosity is a pleasing personality _____.
21. First, second, _____.
23. Valerie liked the new Woody Allen movie, but Eddie hated _____.
24. Men were not allowed to attend the party; it was for women _____.
25. I was going to ask for _____ pancakes, but I had already had enough.
27. The post office abbreviation for *Pennsylvania* is _____.
29. When the results of the census are published, it will be possible to see the economic, religious and _____ breakdown of the population.
30. When John won the tennis tournament three years in a row, there was no question about his _____ as a tennis player.
33. _____ is the abbreviation for *South Carolina.*
35. While I'm eating, my cat never moves. She just _____ and stares at me.
36. Alexander the Great conquered a _____ empire, from Greece to the borders of India.
38. Because it is difficult to appreciate the significance of the numbers, these _____ display the increase in productivity since 1950.
40. _____, I'm not interested in subscribing to that magazine.
41. _____ is the mark of an infinitive.
42. Jennifer is a friend you can _____ on. She is always dependable.
43. _____, or trinitrotoluene, is a powerful explosive.

DOWN

1. Deborah tends to speak out _____, without thinking about what she's saying or worrying about the consequences.
2. Samir is a student in our class. _____ comes from Lebanon.
3. _____ is a suffix used to form the comparative of adjectives.
4. The opposite of *dry* is _____.
5. Miami is a city in the _____ of Florida.

6. Barbara has a warm and pleasant _____; everyone likes her.
7. Natalie did not have a _____ so she couldn't paint the ceiling.
9. Professor Cook is so forgetful that he is a perfect _____ of the absent-minded professor.
11. Mr. Brewster prefers imported wines from Rumania, but his wife likes the _____ wines of California.
14. London is the largest and most important _____ in England.
15. A word that means "small child" is _____.
19. In order to hit the target, you have to _____ carefully and pull the trigger slowly.
22. The abbreviation for *doctor* is _____.
26. You shouldn't expect _____ results when you go on a diet; you should try to lose weight gradually.
28. There _____ seven days in a week.
29. _____ is a Latin abbreviation which means "and so on."
31. Please _____ me another cup of coffee from the pot.
32. How to reduce the increasing cost of living in the United States is a serious economic and political _____ today.
34. I'm having a party _____ my house this weekend.
35. _____ cut herself badly with a kitchen knife.
37. I have one _____ and three daughters.
38. If you _____ to the store, please buy some fruit.
39. Try to finish this puzzle _____ soon as possible.

Crossword Puzzle 8

Use the following definitions and sentences to solve this crossword puzzle. All the words are from Checklists 13 through 16.

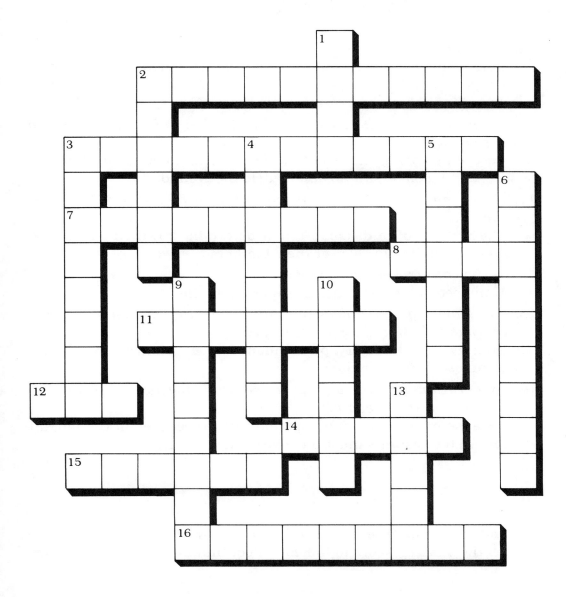

ACROSS

2. *solidly built; large or considerable.*
   Because of the special sale, Ms. Brinker was able to buy a new Volkswagen at a _____ saving.

3. *changing from a country-like to a city-like character.*
Many people are unhappy about the increasing _____ of the countryside and open spaces.

7. *land, usually ruled by a government.*
The Louisiana Purchase of 1803 more than doubled the _____ of the United States.

8. *very small.*
Boris couldn't understand why his English teacher was so upset when he didn't put a period at the end of a sentence. After all, a period is such a _____ mark on paper.

11. *the natural force that attracts objects, that pulls things down to the earth.*
According to legend, Sir Isaac Newton discovered the force of _____ when he saw an apple fall to the ground.

12. *either male or female; all living things are divided into one or the other.*
The _____ of birds can often be determined by their size, shape and especially the color of their feathers.

14. *of the countryside; not urban.*
Many people prefer _____ life to urban life.

15. *any teaching which does not agree with the church or what is commonly believed by most people.*
In early church history, punishment for _____ was much more common than it is today.

16. *concerning mechanical or practical skill; specialized in a trade, profession, science, etc.*
Because of the special equipment and procedures in the lab, all research assistants must have very fine _____ skills.

DOWN

1. *facts taken as true, the starting point for analysis.*
All the _____ seem to indicate a continuing rise in the inflation rate.

2. *an area of many homes near a large metropolitan area.*
Margaret doesn't want to live in a large city. She enjoys living in a _____ because it is far enough from the noise of the city, but close enough for shopping and entertainment.

3. *final, last; greatest, furthest.*
Mr. Vartan's _____ aim is to become the executive of a large import-export company.

4. *the time between events, or the space between two things.*
Because Veronica didn't understand what was said to her, there was an embarrassing _____ of several seconds before she spoke.

5. *clear, evident; something that is easily seen or understood.*
Nelson is very fat. It is _____ that he eats too much and should go on a diet.

6. *one who practices medicine; a doctor.*
Alicia plans to study medicine so she can become a _____ in the rural villages of her country.

9. *a small part, or a piece broken off.*
If Evelyn had all the broken pieces, she could glue the dish together again but a single _____ was missing and could not be found.

10. *a state of affairs; position or rank.*
Professor Dresner's report on the _____ of women in management positions would have been discouraging had she not offered many valuable suggestions.

13. *the art of seeming to make things happen outside of the laws of nature.*
All the children enjoyed watching Marmaduke the Magician perform his amazing _____.

Review Test 1

Select the one word from the four choices that best completes the sentence. Write *the correct form of the word* on the line at the right.

1. Researchers have found a definite _____ between the hours of preparation for an exam and the exam grade. _____

   anecdote   correlate ·   propose   respond

2. Because of his horrible behavior in school, the principal decided that Jerry needed special _____, but no teacher was willing to accept the responsibility. _____

   devastate   transcend   initiate   supervise

3. When Sylvia's father died, her boyfriend was the first to _____ her. _____

   confirm   console   commit   invert

4. Because the cathedral walls were no longer strong, they had to be _____ with steel and stone. _____

   contribution   expansion   reinforcement   liberation

5. Willie's mother asked him for _____ that he had not been smoking behind the garage. _____

   assist   assurance   modify   transfer

6. To be excused from any required course, a student must write a detailed _____ to the department head. _____

   motive   grant   label   appeal

7. Many words in English are _____ from Latin. _____

   devise   derive   assume   imply

8. The weather was so rainy and cold this morning that I would have never _____ that it would be so beautiful this afternoon. _____

   induce   predict   prevail   infer

9. The prisoner's hand moved so slowly toward the key that his movement was _____ to the guard. _____

unalterable   unavailable   imperceptible   irrational

10. The manager asked the teen-agers to leave the club because membership was _____ to people over 30. _____

integration   rejection   restriction   conversion

11. At last night's concert, the audience _____ in age from 19 to 75. _____

ally   impel   obtain   range

12. The _____ of metric measurements to English measurements is not difficult, but some people have difficulty doing it. _____

affect   convert   propose   frustrate

13. A _____ from every person, no matter how small or insignificant, will help the Red Cross reach its goal of $250,000. _____

contract   concentrate   contribute   construct

14. The artist had set up his studio so that it would be _____ as work space and comfortable as living space. _____

function   theory   section   disproportion

15. Banks usually charge a small fee to _____ one currency to another. _____

acquire   convert   segregate   insist

16. Because the house was _____, the children enjoyed playing hide and seek in the empty rooms. _____

adapt   maintain   abandon   proceed

17. When one travels to a foreign country, the change of language, food, climate and customs requires a great deal of _____. _____

assure   adjust   imply   infer

18. Big Bruce ate a dozen hamburgers in the _____ time of four and a half minutes. _____

    incredible   economic   incredulous   economical

19. The _____ in temperature – very high during the day and very low at night – caused Janet a great deal of discomfort. _____

    coordinate   rely   vary   stimulate

20. The author cleverly kept the reader guessing. The solution to the crime was not _____ until the very last page. _____

    exclude   reveal   estimate   persist

21. Unemployment and the cost of living are the only _____ in the campaign on which the candidates agree. _____

    images   plots   issues   contacts

22. The chance of a government scholarship was all the _____ that Hazel needed to study hard. _____

    exertion   motivation   vision   credibility

23. Although the prisoner would not speak, the judge interpreted his silence as a _____ confession of guilt. _____

    tiny   beneficial   virtual   vacant

24. The two groups faced wide disagreement. In fact, their viewpoints were so _____ that there seemed no chance at all to reach agreement. _____

    polarize   estimate   neutralize   deductible

25. The doctors were convinced that the baby was physically normal, but they suspected that she was mentally _____. _____

    adaptable   abnormal   exclusive   sufficient

Review Test 2

Below are 25 adjectives. On the blank line in the following phrases, write the *negative* form of the adjective. The first is done for you as an example.

stable   an <u>unstable</u> person

1. available   a boss who is _____

2. capable   _____ of doing anything well

3. comprehensible   an _____ language

4. consistent   a very _____ argument

5. normal   unhappy parents of the _____ child

6. similar   three quite _____ brothers

7. intelligent   a slow, _____ student

8. definite   an _____ answer

9. inhabitable   a very old, _____ house

10. integrated   an ancient, _____ castle wall

11. distinct   an _____ finger print

12. cooperative   a student who is _____

13. efficient   an _____ method of studying

14. legal   an _____ search of the house

15. personal   a distant, _____ smile

16. secure   a frightened, _____ feeling

17. impressive   an _____ record of attendance

18. rational   a confused, _____ reply

19. logical   a disconnected, _____ argument

20. conventional   a person with _____ habits

21. visible   a tiny, almost _____ scratch

22. reliable   a machine that is _____

23. sufficient   _____ time for relaxation

24. constitutional   an _____ law

25. significant   a small, _____ mistake

Review Test 3

For each underlined word in the following phrases, choose one of the four words or phrases which is closest in meaning. Circle the word or phrase. The first is done for you as an example.

an <u>unintelligent</u> remark
necessary   (stupid)   predictable   amusing

1. an <u>instant</u> success
   unexpected   momentary   ultimate   immediate

2. a <u>rural</u> town
   metropolitan   central   country   regional

3. a <u>tiny</u> insect
   small   dangerous   flying   hungry

4. a <u>positive</u> answer
   negative   irrelevant   final   affirmative

5. an <u>odd</u> occurrence
   spontaneous   unusual   frightening   similar

6. an <u>ultimate</u> goal
   attainable   subjective   final   empirical

7. a <u>previous</u> occasion
   earlier   satisfying   formal   serious

8. <u>divine</u> services
   ordinary   expensive   restricted   religious

9. <u>alternative</u> plans
   inefficient   other   previous   changed

10. the <u>primary</u> purpose
    old-fashioned   most recent   neglected   main

11. a <u>capable</u> person
    able   wealthy   angry   frustrated

12. a <u>liberal</u> allowance
    restrictive   insufficient   generous   indefinite

13. a <u>secure</u> place
    medical   safe   religious   important

14. a <u>specific</u> amount
    predictable   excessive   exact   superior

15. a <u>subjective</u> decision
    personal   intelligent   uncertain   unreasonable

16. a <u>vast</u> amount of money
    immense   estimated   tiny   required

17. a <u>subtle</u> smell of perfume
    very fashionable   attractive   hardly noticeable   unpleasant

18. an <u>initial</u> reaction
    first   final   military   impulsive

19. an <u>erroneous</u> conclusion
    undistinguished   irrational   wrong   logical

20. <u>incessant</u> rain
    tropical   without stopping   by the seashore   unexpected

21. the <u>authorized</u> version
    officially approved   edited and revised   written by several authors
           illegally printed

22. an <u>insignificant</u> person
    uninformed   dissatisfied   unimportant   non-governmental

23. a <u>potential</u> victory
    hopeful   powerful   important   possible

24. an <u>impulsive</u> act
    spontaneous   intellectual   analytical   deliberate

25. a <u>grave</u> matter
    deadly   serious   expensive   temporary

Review Test 4

Select the one word from the four choices that best completes the sentence. Write the *correct form of the word* on the line at the right.

1. There is no _____ difference in meaning between the words *a gift* and *a present*.   _____

    similar   significant   obligatory   magnificent

2. Christina told her husband to _____ himself as if he were a gentleman, even though he isn't.   _____

    conduct   feature   mobilize   assume

3. Grandpa Green bought an illustrated _____ of *Lady Chatterley's Lover*.   _____

    heresy   factor   repression   edition

4. Because his pronunciation is so bad, many people cannot _____ Ahmed when he speaks.   _____

    coincidence   comprehension   modification   attribute

5. Many old people, now called "senior citizens," _____ Senator Doddard for voting against the old age pension.   _____

    duplicate   denounce   perceive   transcend

6. If Bernice says something is black, her husband will _____ her and say it is white.   _____

    convert   exclude   contradict   dictate

7. When Harvey's teacher congratulated him for his good score on the vocabulary test, he studied the next lesson even harder. He always responds to the _____ of praise.   _____

    instinct   impulse   stimulate   ratio

8. Twenty years ago the city started to rebuild the sixteenth-century cathedral, and now the _____ is complete.   _____

    momentum   restoration   obligation   proposition

9. Mr. O'Grady was afraid that he might set a _____ if he wore his Bermuda shorts to church. _____

precedent   proportion   summary   vacancy

10. Gordon was happy to hear that he had _____ three cats, two birds and a goldfish when his Aunt Agatha died. _____

testify   suppress   inhabit   inherit

11. Of all the countries in the world, China is the largest in population and the U.S.S.R. is the largest in _____. _____

area   perspective   proportion   technology

12. Because she has trained so hard and so long, my grandmother is a _____ winner in the Grandparents' Motorcycle Race. _____

subordination   circumstance   potential   coherence

13. Although he understands his wife well, Judson hasn't any _____ at all why she enjoys roller skating so much. _____

data   issue   norm   notion

14. In any argument between her parents, Helen tries to remain _____. _____

visible   neutral   subtle   hostile

15. During World War II, Germany and Italy were _____. _____

allies   analogies   immigrants   orbits

16. The secretary _____ pressure by telephoning all the committee members and asking for their support. _____

impel   unify   constitute   exert

17. Many childhood diseases, such as measles and mumps, are _____ and easily spread among students in school. _____

contagious   acquired   cultural   ethnic

18. The _____ of the cold in the Arctic is so great that the temperature sometimes drops to −50° F. _____

variety   intensity   interval   range

19. In order to travel outside of your country, you must have a _____ passport. _____

specify   validate   encode   devote

20. Frequently the fog is so _____ around San Francisco that you cannot see the Golden Gate Bridge. _____

density   abstraction   function   derivation

21. It's hard to believe that Sam wants to be an accountant. He can't even add _____. _____

secure   accurate   obvious   acute

22. When Esther dropped the glass, it shattered into dozens of tiny _____. _____

fragments   destructions   factors   proportions

23. It's _____ that keeps us from flying off the earth into space. _____

hypotheses   gravity   migrations   physiology

24. Cynthia and Bill had never been especially friendly, but they had never been _____ either. _____

adjustable   hostile   delinquent   heretical

25. Many people are unhappy about the increasing _____ of the countryside and open spaces. _____

territory   significance   environment   urbanization

Final Review Crossword Puzzle

Use the following definitions and sentences to solve this crossword puzzle. All of the words are from the Checklists.

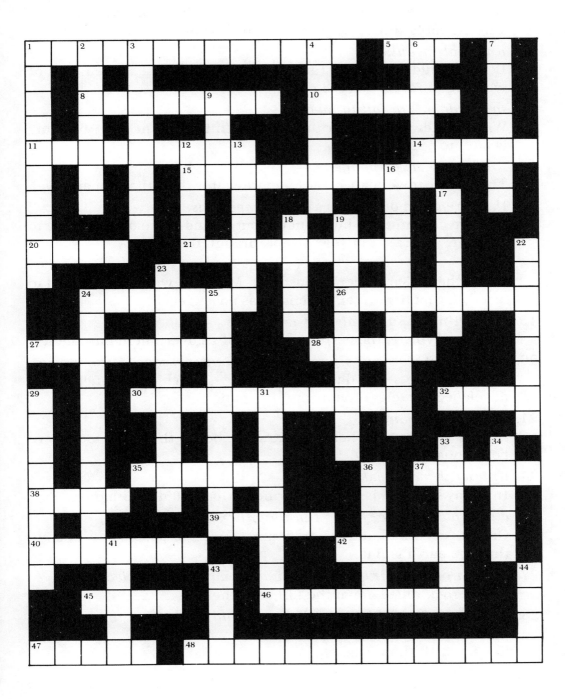

ACROSS

1. *all the surrounding conditions that affect the development of a person, animal or plant (adjective).*
   Many people today have _____ concerns, such as the purity of water, anti-pollution devices for automobiles and factories, preventing forest fires and protecting our wildlife.

5. *unusual; peculiar.*
   Louise could not understand her husband's _____ behavior of wearing different-colored socks.

8. *to fall down; to fall to pieces.*
   Without new support or additional reinforcement, that building is sure to _____.

10. *to soak up, as a sponge.*
    This paper towel can _____ more water than that paper towel.

11. *the spreading of ideas, rumors or feelings.*
    The fire continued to burn out of control and, from one building to another, a _____ of fear swept through the area.

14. *legal.*
    When the police officer stopped her, Mrs. Asti was embarrassed to discover that her driver's license was no longer _____.

15. *something or someone that is typical.*
    Senator Irving is the perfect _____ of a government bureaucrat.

20. *a system of words or signals used to send messages, often secret.*
    A series of dots and dashes was a _____ which Samuel Morse developed for telegraphic communication.

21. *mistaken; wrong.*
    At one time people held the _____ belief that tomatoes were poisonous.

24. *unlawful; not legal.*
    In many states, it is _____ for liquor to be sold on Sundays.

26. *a group of people; fewer than another group.*
    Only a very small and insignificant _____ of people now believe that the earth is flat.

27. *motion of a moving object (equal to mass times velocity).*
    As the rock rolled down the hill, it gathered _____.

28. *a manner of speaking, writing, dressing, painting, etc.*
    Hernando's teacher claimed that his writing _____ was more like Spanish than English.

30. *splendid, grand.*
    Peter and Dorothy were reminded of their honeymoon when they
    saw the _____ sunrise over the lake.

32. *an amount of space within boundaries.*
    Judith's little boy never wants to stay within his own play _____.

35. *position or rank.*
    The _____ of teachers in many countries is below that of doc-
    tors, engineers and politicians.

37. *an almost unnoticeable quantity of something.*
    Kathy found a _____ of sodium in the solution when she an-
    alyzed it.

38. *to prepare written material for publication by making changes
    and corrections*
    As news editor for the television station, one of my responsibilities
    is to _____ the content of news programs.

39. *the countryside; a farming rather than an industrial area.*
    The Morgans prefer living in a _____ environment to living in a
    suburban or metropolitan area.

40. *made up of.*
    The poetic form of a sonnet, by definition, has to _____ of
    fourteen lines.

42. *to travel in a curved path while moving in space.*
    John Glenn was the first American astronaut to _____ the
    earth.

45. *a real or imaginary straight line on which something rotates.*
    The earth rotates on its _____ every twenty-four hours.

46. *outer; on, coming from or applied to the outside.*
    The opposite of *internal* is _____.

47. *stop.*
    Her baby's incessant crying bothered the mother but nothing she
    did caused the noise to _____.

48. *supposed to be true but not yet proved (adverb).*
    To avoid an argument about the facts, the professor spoke _____
    about the subject.

DOWN

1. *working well with the least effort or waste.*
   Because Randy does not allow any distractions, such as radio or
   television, his _____ while studying is very great.

2. *a room, apartment or house for rent.*
   As soon as the boarder moved out of his rented room, the _____ was advertised in the newspaper.

3. *dependable, suitable to be trusted.*
   Jerry believes everything his wife tells him because her information is so _____.

4. *to leave forever.*
   The refugees had to _____ their homes and flee from the area.

6. *to get or obtain.*
   A person can _____ a great deal of pleasure from an interesting hobby.

7. *to make certain; to assure the truth.*
   When I called to _____ my seat on the 8:00 flight to Rio de Janeiro, I was told that the flight had been cancelled.

9. *the main story in a novel or play.*
   The _____ of the story was so complicated, with so many different characters, that I did not finish reading the novel.

12. *a matter of immediate interest or discussion.*
    My sixteen-year-old brother does not understand why it's such a big _____ in my house if he comes home past midnight.

13. *not on either side of a dispute.*
    Not wanting to favor either side, Mildred tried to remain _____ during the argument between her son and daughter.

16. *the character and behavior of a person which make him or her different from other people.*
    Ms. Graham told her students that an English composition which is vague and confused usually reflects the _____ of the writer.

17. *to state or declare.*
    Although the criminal was obviously guilty, he tried to _____ his innocence.

18. *combined into one; joined together.*
    During the American Revolution, Benjamin Franklin argued for _____, telling the revolutionists that if they didn't all hang together, they would surely hang separately.

19. *a promise or responsibility to someone or some course of action.*
    Some people feel that marriage is the most important _____ a person can make.

22. *referring to the human body.*
    The doctor's examination showed that Aunt Cecilia, despite her age, was in excellent _____ condition.

23. *noun form of 13* DOWN.
Switzerland has managed to maintain its _____ through many wars.

24. *movement of a settler from his or her own country to another.*
_____ to the United States from Europe was highest at the beginning of the twentieth century.

25. *to give out, to be in charge of.*
Even though my mother was never able to _____ any kind of punishment to us children, we grew up respecting her authority.

29. *something that gives proof.*
When faced with the _____ of his fingerprints, the thief could not deny his guilt.

31. *to prevent something from happening.*
It looks as though bad weather is going to _____ our plans for a picnic this weekend.

33. *adjective form of 42* ACROSS.
The moon travels in an _____ path around the earth.

34. *to happen.*
Next year Leslie's birthday will _____ on February 29th.

36. *a feeling of great fear (adjective).*
Beverly does not like to watch _____ movies, like the old Frankenstein films, because they are so frightening.

41. *the characteristic of being male or female (plural).*
Nobody has ever won what some humorists call "The Battle of the _____."

43. *a country or person joined together with another for a common purpose.*
During World War II the United States was the _____ of England.

44. *to depend on; trust.*
Richard could always _____ on his wife to help him prepare dinner.

Answer Key

Exercise 1

1. conclusion
2. contradict
3. constructed
4. restricted
5. instruction
6. rejected
7. edit
8. invaded
9. exerted
10. selected
11. abstract
12. prediction
13. emit
14. project
15. assert
16. contractions
17. contradictory
18. exclusive
19. contract
20. expand
21. instruction
22. invasion
23. convert
24. comprehension
25. constructed

Exercise 2

1. contribution
2. initial
3. estimate
4. devotion
5. coordinate
6. communication
7. duplicate
8. correlation
9. devastated
10. executive
11. devotee
12. concentrate
13. dominant
14. formulate
15. devout/devoted
16. attributed
17. demonstration
18. demonstrators
19. demonstrative
20. frustration(s)
21. frustrated
22. frustrating
23. initiated
24. initiative
25. initial

Exercise 3

1. motivation
2. asserted
3. investigate
4. stimulant
5. repress
6. insubordinate
7. supervise
8. integration/ desegregation
9. retained
10. isolated
11. deduce
12. expose
13. obligation
14. suppress
15. impressed
16. radiation
17. participant
18. Immigration
19. immigrant
20. emigrated
21. migration
22. emigration
23. deduce
24. inductive
25. deduce

Exercise 4

1. derives
2. derivation
3. implicit
4. implied
5. implication
6. identification
7. identity
8. identical
9. modification(s)
10. various
11. evolved
12. interpretations
13. restoration
14. specific
15. interpret
16. implicit/ implied
17. adapt
18. condense
19. acquisition
20. alterations
21. conformity
22. incessant
23. conserve
24. proposition
25. indefinitely

Exercise 5

1. inherit
2. heritage
3. hereditary
4. persistence
5. persistently
6. persisted
7. reliance
8. reliable
9. rely
10. ignore
11. precedent
12. assistance
13. adhere
14. correspond
15. maintain
16. assured
17. coherence
18. adhesive
19. ignored
20. transcend
21. occurrence
22. implication
23. inferred
24. implied
25. inference

Exercise 6

1. achievement
2. adjust
3. abandon
4. reinforced
5. commit
6. inconceivable
7. accompany
8. inducement
9. imperceptible
10. perceptive
11. perception
12. perceived
13. involved
14. involvement
15. conception
16. conceive
17. inconceivable
18. assumed
19. absorb
20. obtainable
21. accomplishment
22. adjustable
23. attained
24. required
25. established

Exercise 7

1. synthetics
2. irrational
3. mobile
4. critical
5. normalize
6. intellectualize
7. polarized
8. economical
9. emphatically
10. abnormal
11. criticism
12. visualize
13. economics
14. authority
15. polar
16. instability
17. rationally
18. dramatist
19. emphasis
20. emphasize
21. emphatic
22. emphatically
23. theory
24. theoretically
25. theoretician

Exercise 8

1. bombarded
2. design
3. diagrammed
4. feature
5. appealed
6. dispute
7. compound
8. aid
9. financial
10. avail
11. conflicts
12. alliance
13. beneficial
14. dispute
15. conduct
16. contacts
17. unavailable
18. contrast
19. collapse
20. unapproachable
21. conductor
22. financier
23. benefactor
24. undisputed/indisputable
25. collapsible

Exercise 9

1. issue
2. trace
3. shift
4. label(s)
5. interview
6. orbit
7. plot
8. functional
9. range
10. rebelled
11. process
12. transferred
13. released
14. research
15. release
16. laboriously
17. tortured
18. phase
19. shifts
20. label
21. grant
22. issue
23. transferable
24. rebellious
25. plot

Exercise 10

1. affected
2. affection
3. elaborate
4. alternative
5. coincidence
6. analytically
7. distinctive
8. Inconsistent
9. commune
10. consists
11. deny
12. device
13. distinguish
14. analyzed
15. conventionally
16. approximately
17. assembly
18. affectation
19. code
20. erroneous
21. horror
22. analysis
23. deny
24. distinct
25. devise

Exercise 11

1. inhabited
2. prosperity
3. secure
4. validity
5. uniform
6. intensify
7. succession
8. liberal
9. responsive
10. inverse
11. vacant
12. procedure
13. liberalize
14. uninhabitable
15. inhabitant
16. prevails
17. prevalence
18. prevalent
19. sufficient
20. insufficient
21. suffice
22. impulse
23. publicity
24. majority
25. testimony

Exercise 12

1. accuracy
2. Contrary
3. crisis
4. density
5. consequences
6. adulthood
7. analogy
8. inappropriate
9. circumstantial
10. constant
11. delinquency
12. inefficient
13. contagious
14. anecdotes
15. capable
16. aggression
17. complex
18. consequence
19. contagion
20. circumstances
21. incredible
22. incredulously
23. incredulity
24. credibility
25. credible

Exercise 13

1. methodical
2. physiological
3. fragment
4. environmental
5. instinctively
6. impersonal
7. heretical
8. imperialistic
9. periodic
10. logic
11. energetic
12. phenomenon
13. empirical
14. objective
15. methodical
16. evidence
17. final
18. personal
19. hostile
20. miraculously
21. miraculous
22. miracle
23. precise
24. precision
25. precisely

Exercise 14

1. proportion
2. subjective
3. responsibility
4. spontaneous
5. radical
6. psychological
7. urban
8. styles
9. substantial
10. primary
11. subtle
12. potential
13. sex
14. territory
15. technical
16. tone
17. topic
18. vast
19. disproportionate
20. suicidal
21. traditionally
22. province
23. Primitive
24. superior
25. impotent

Exercise 15

1. attitude
2. factors
3. status
4. principle
5. sources
6. momentum
7. monarchy
8. interval
9. trend
10. spectrum
11. instance
12. area
13. doctrine
14. stereotype
15. morale
16. currency
17. perspective
18. trait
19. axis
20. ratio
21. data
22. version
23. momentum
24. status
25. equilibrium

Exercise 16

1. obvious	10. odd	19. virtually
2. virtual	11. acute	20. ultimately
3. instantly	12. previous	21. negative
4. positive	13. domestically	22. previous
5. external	14. illegally	23. divine
6. ethnic	15. tiny	24. domestic
7. imperative	16. supreme	25. instantly
8. negatively	17. legal	
9. rural	18. acute	

Review Test 1

1. correlation	10. restricted	19. variation
2. supervision	11. ranged	20. revealed
3. console	12. conversion	21. issues
4. reinforced	13. contribution	22. motivation
5. assurance	14. functional	23. virtual
6. appeal	15. convert	24. polarized
7. derived	16. abandoned	25. abnormal
8. predicted	17. adjustment	
9. imperceptible	18. incredible	

Review Test 2

1. unavailable	10. disintegrated	19. illogical
2. incapable	11. indistinct	20. unconventional
3. incomprehensible	12. uncooperative	21. invisible
4. inconsistent	13. inefficient	22. unreliable
5. abnormal	14. illegal	23. insufficient
6. dissimilar	15. impersonal	24. unconstitutional
7. unintelligent	16. insecure	25. insignificant
8. indefinite	17. unimpressive	
9. uninhabitable	18. irrational	

Review Test 3

1. immediate
2. country
3. small
4. affirmative
5. unusual
6. final
7. earlier
8. religious
9. other
10. main
11. able
12. generous
13. safe
14. exact
15. personal
16. immense
17. hardly noticeable
18. first
19. wrong
20. without stopping
21. officially approved
22. unimportant
23. possible
24. spontaneous
25. serious

Review Test 4

1. significant
2. conduct
3. edition
4. comprehend
5. denounced
6. contradict
7. stimulus
8. restoration
9. precedent
10. inherited
11. area
12. potential
13. notion
14. neutral
15. allies
16. exerted
17. contagious
18. intensity
19. valid/validated
20. dense
21. accurately
22. fragments
23. gravity
24. hostile
25. urbanization

Answer Key
to Crossword Puzzles

Crossword Puzzle 1

Crossword Puzzle 2

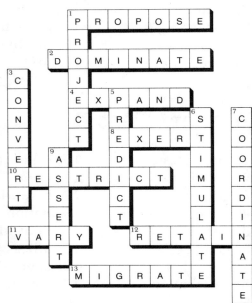

Crossword Puzzle 3

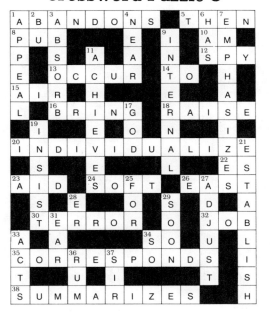

Crossword Puzzle 4

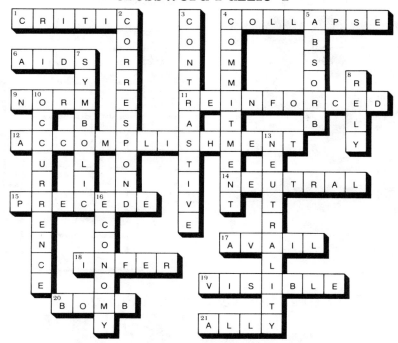

Crossword Puzzle 5

Crossword Puzzle 6

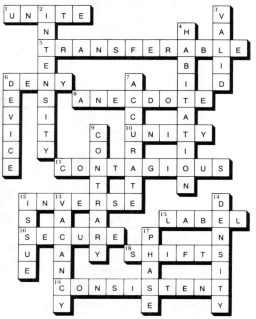

Crossword Puzzle 7

Crossword Puzzle 8

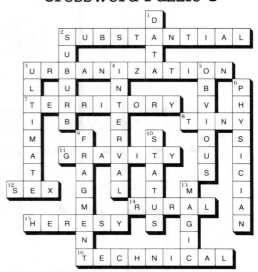

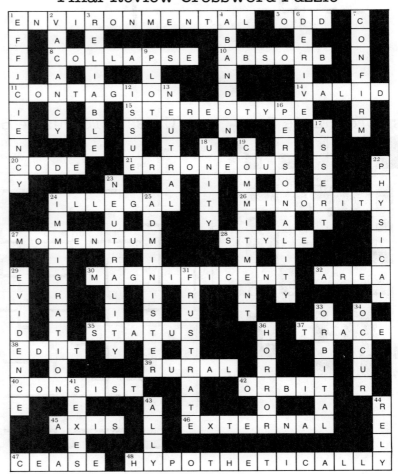

Final Review Crossword Puzzle

Index of Base Words

initiate 2
insist 5
instance 15
instant 16
instinct 13
institute 2
instruct 1
integrate 3
intellectual 7
intensify 11
internalize 7
interpret 4
interval 15
interview 9
invade 1
invert 11
investigate 3
involve 6
isolate 3
issue 9

justify 4

label 9
labor 9
legal 16
liberal 11
liberate 11
logic 13

magic 13
magnificent 13
magnitude 13
maintain 5
major 11
method 13
metropolis 13
migrate 3
military 13
minor 13
misinterpret 4
miracle 13
mobilize 7
modify 4
momentum 15
monarch 15
morale 15
motivate 3

negative 16
neutral 7
norm 7
notion 13

objective 13
obligate 3
oblige 3
obtain 6
obvious 16
occur 5
odd 16
orbit 9

participate 3
perceive 6
perception 6
period 13
persist 5
personality 13
perspective 15
phase 9
phenomenon 13
philosophy 7
physical 13
physician 13
physiology 13
physique 13
plot 9
pole 7
portion 14
positive 16
potential 14
precede 5
precise 13
predict 1
predominant 2
prevail 11
previous 16
prime 14
principle 15
proceed 11
process 9
project 1
proportion 14
propose 4
prosper 11
province 14
psychology 14

publicize 11
publish 11

radiate 3
radical 14
range 9
ratio 15
rationalize 7
rebel 9
region 13
reinforce 6
reject 1
release 9
rely 5
repress 3
require 6
research 9
respond 11
responsibility 14
restore 4
restrict 1
retain 3
reveal 4
revise 3
revolt 4
revolution 4
rural 16

section 14
secure 11
segregate 3
select 1
serial 14
series 14
sex 14
shift 9
significance 5
signify 5
similarity 13
source 15
specify 4
spectrum 15
sphere 14
spontaneous 14
stabilize 7
status 15
stereotype 15
stimulate 3
structure 14

style 14
subjective 14
subordinate 3
substance 14
subtle 14
suburb 14
succeed 11
successor 11
sufficient 11
suicide 14
summary 7
superior 14
supervise 3
suppress 3
supreme 16
symbol 7
synthetic 7

technical 14
technique 14
technology 14
territory 14
terror 7
testify 11
testimony 11
theory 7
tiny 16
tone 14
topic 14
torture 9
trace 9
tradition 14
trait 15
transcend 5
transfer 9
trend 15

ultimate 16
unify 11
unity 11
urban 14

vacate 11
valid 11
vary 4
vast 14
version 15
virtual 16
visible 7
vision 7